The Boston Globe

This book is available in quantity at special discounts
for your group or organization. For further information, contact:
Triumph Books
542 South Dearborn Street, Suite 750
Chicago, Illinois 60605
Phone: (312) 939-3330
Fax: (312) 663-3557

Printed in the United States of America
ISBN-13: 978-1-57243-895-8
ISBN-10: 1-57243-895-9

TRIUMPH BOOKS
CHICAGO

COVER PHOTOGRAPHS

FRONT, CLOCKWISE FROM UPPER LEFT:
Skate chowder, Boston Globe photo/ Pam Berry; crabs from Deer Isle, Maine, Boston Globe photo/ Janet Knott; lobster from Boston's Locke-Ober restaurant,
Boston Globe photo/ Wendy Maeda; clams from Duxbury Beach, Massachusetts, Boston Globe photo/ Barry Chin.
BACK:
Former Red Sox great Carl Yastrzemski hooks a striped bass near Plum Island, Massachusetts. Boston Globe photo/ Stan Grossfeld.

NEW ENGLAND
Seafood
COOKBOOK

FOREWORD BY JASPER WHITE
INTRODUCTION BY SHERYL JULIAN AND JULIE RIVEN

Contents

Contributors

Many talented people lent their culinary expertise to the pages of this book.
Here are just a few key names to know going in:

Some people think that food editor **SHERYL JULIAN** has the best job at The Boston Globe. Her office is filled with samples of the latest nutrition bars, sodas, chocolates, and popcorn. Most weeks, the stack of review cookbooks comes up to her waist. "The problem," she says, "is that most of the foods don't taste very good." And the books? "They're a huge distraction." But what tastes and sounds good gets a spot in the paper's weekly Food section.
This Cordon Bleu-trained cook has won several national awards for writing. She began the Boston Globe Magazine's "Cooking" column more than 20 years ago and asked photographer Jim

Scherer to work with her when she met him through the late Julia Child. Now she writes and styles food with Julie Riven. The two are co-authors of "The Way We Cook" (Houghton Mifflin), their celebration of cooking at home.

JULIE RIVEN has faced tough audiences. When she was the cook for hundreds of teenage boys at the Roxbury Latin School in Massachusetts, they let her know – in no uncertain terms – what they liked and didn't like. "After teenage boys, you can cook for anyone," she says. "And they didn't even mind when I stirred fresh corn kernels into their bowls of spicy chili." In fact, they named her

kitchen the "Ritz Roxbury."
Formerly a high-risk obstetrics nurse, Riven attended the Cambridge School of Culinary Arts and honed her cooking skills in superstar chef Todd English's first Boston-area kitchen at Michela's restaurant. For the last dozen years, she and "The Way We Cook" co-author Sheryl Julian have co-written the Boston Globe Magazine's popular "Cooking" column, and co-styled food for Jim Scherer's handsome accompanying photographs.

When **JIM SCHERER** nails a shot, he knows it, because people lick their lips and mumble, "Mmm." Scherer photographs

food, something he's been doing freelance for The Boston Globe for more than 20 years. "If I've succeeded, I've done two things: created a picture that's visually appealing, but the other thing is creating a visceral, gut reaction," he explains. "Everybody is interested in food. You look at a food picture, and you're immediately hungry. That's awesome."
Like so many who work with food in Boston, he owes a debt to Julia Child, who introduced him to food photography, then had him shoot three of her cookbooks. As for why he loves photographing food, he says a lobster roll, unlike a person, doesn't need to be told where to stand. On the other hand, food never comes out the same twice. "It takes strong teamwork," he says. Plus, he gets to sample. "That's definitely a great perk."

In six years of food writing, **JOE YONAN** has interviewed many famous authors and killed his own chicken for dinner. He's also tagged along as the world's biggest Chowhound ate his way through suburban Massachusetts, five Italian chefs hunted for pheasant in New Hampshire, and a houseful of Boston college students ordered from four delivery services simultaneously. For The Boston Globe's monthly "Gadgets" column, he tests the small (vegetable peelers), the big (gas and charcoal grills), and most everything in between. A West Texas native, he is a 2000 graduate of the Cambridge School of Culinary Arts in Massachusetts.

PETER KELLY knows that unless you have your own cooking show, the kitchen, like an egg roll, may be full of mystery. Canola or olive oil? Why do recipes specify 'unsalted butter,' and then include salt in the ingredients? The Boston Globe's "Ask the Cooks" column provides answers. And when the Globe's resident cook, Sheryl Julian, and "Cooking" coauthor Julie Riven aren't fielding the question, it falls to Kelly, a chef and instructor at Johnson & Wales University in Providence, Rhode Island.

An avid marathon runner and published poet, Kelly answers the butter question this way: "If you think of something like mashed potatoes, ... it would take a huge amount of butter to do the work of a teaspoon or so of salt. This illustration should answer the question, don't you think?" We do.

Ever wished for a virtual taste of your favorite chef's favorite dishes? Since its inception in 1999, BOSTONCHEFS.COM has been providing food fans with a fun and functional showcase of the city's finest culinary talents. The site offers a vibrant guide to Boston dining, with mouth-watering food photos, menus, recipes, chef bios, culinary news, and events. All of which makes BostonChefs.com the perfect source for our "Celebrity Catch" features, highlighting the recipes of Jasper White, Lydia Shire, Ken Oringer, Jody Adams, Gordon Hamersley, and Ana Sortun. You'll find their signature dishes at the end of each chapter in this book. And on the web, of course: Visit www.BostonChefs.com.

Book Staff

EDITOR Janice Page
ART DIRECTOR/DESIGNER Rena Anderson Sokolow
ASSOCIATE EDITOR Andrea Pyenson
COPY EDITOR Ann Cortissoz
RESEARCHERS Ben Cafardo, Meghann Gregory, Leah Putnam, Lisa Tuite
IMAGING Frank Bright

Photographers

Pam Berry, 61, 62 • John Blanding, 30, 56 • Dominic Chavez, 82 • Fred J. Field, 138 • Bill Greene, 50 • Pat Greenhouse, 71, 102 • Tom Herde, 60, 106 • Janet Knott, 17, 18, 44, 95, 118 • Suzanne Krelter, 8 • Tom Landers, 142 Wendy Maeda, 28, 54, 99 • Michele McDonald, 29, 70 Lisa Poole, 70 • Joanne Rathe, 40, 115 • Evan Richman, 114 • Jim Scherer, 23, 26, 34, 36, 37, 38, 46, 68, 76, 86, 92, 98, 104, 113, 124, 128, 131, 134 • Paul Schiavone, 11, 33, 53, 73, 101, 121, 137 • Shawn Thew, 2 • John Tlumacki, 74, 111 • Carl Tremblay, 88 • Lane Turner, 6, 20, 31 Jonathan Wiggs, 117, 122 • Mark Wilson, 16

Photo Stylists

Sheryl Julian and Julie Riven, 23, 26, 34, 36, 37, 38, 46, 56, 68, 76, 86, 88, 92, 98, 104, 113, 124, 128, 131, 134

Additional Contributors

Jody Adams, Alison Arnett, Letitia Baldwin, Rachel Ellner, Keri Fisher, Gordon Hamersley, Jonathan Levitt, Honor Lydon, Alan Lupo, Ken Oringer, Ken Rivard, Steven Rosenberg, Debra Samuels, Emily Schwab, Jan Shepherd, Lydia Shire, Clea Simon, Ana Sortun, Sarah Tomlinson, Ted Weesner Jr., Catherine Walthers, Jasper White, Lisa Zwirn

With special thanks to The Boston Globe Food section and Sunday Magazine

Foreword

BY JASPER WHITE

Most people think of me as a seafood chef. It definitely is my specialty. But it was never a conscious decision on my part.

My first job in Boston was chef at the Cafe Plaza in the Copley Plaza Hotel back in 1979. I had spent several years working around the country in fine dining establishments where poultry, veal, lamb, beef, and game far outsold seafood. It was the city of Boston and my customers that made me a seafood chef, because in Boston, seafood is the dominant part of our dining culture.

When people used to ask me where to find the best seafood in town, my stock answer would be "wherever the best chefs are cooking." (Now I tell them to come to the Summer Shack, my group of casual seafood restaurants.) The truth is that in Boston and all around New England, good seafood is everywhere, and it takes many forms. It can be found at clam shacks, pubs, casual neighborhood restaurants, ethnic eateries, and fine dining establishments. But good seafood isn't just for dining out; it's also part of the repertoire of many home cooks.

Yes, people actually cook seafood at home here in New England, from clam pie and oyster stew to seared haddock with caramelized parsnips. I know, because I talk to folks who use my recipes all the time, and they ask me very savvy questions, many of which are answered on the following user-friendly pages.

I can't think of a team that has been more influential in teaching New England home cooks about preparing seafood than the writers at The Boston Globe, including food editor Sheryl Julian and her long-time collaborator, Julie Riven. Week after week, they offer us new recipes and ideas, along with old standards that are given new twists. They also provide good basic cooking lessons on traditional local dishes such as boiled lobster and steamers. And they publish recipes from great home cooks living in the area, as well as signature dishes from culinary stars.

This book reflects all of that knowledge and coverage, but it's not intended to be a stuffy treatise on seafood. It's more like a box full of favorite clippings from some of Boston's best food writers and creative local chefs.

And it's about New England's wonderful ingredients. Look at the clams on the cover — locally grown, which I can tell by their steel color. The rest of the country thinks hard-shell clams are white, but we know they don't turn chalky white until they've been out of the water for a couple of days.

The reason that seafood cooking is so prevalent in New England is because it's a mecca for the seafood industry. Granted, our resources have dwindled since the turn of the last century, when more than 80 fishing vessels would bring about 1 million pounds of seafood to the Boston Fish Pier each day. But the Fish Pier and surrounding South Boston area are still home to many seafood businesses clustered together like computer companies in Silicon Valley. Here fish and shellfish come by land, sea, and air from fishing ports throughout New England and maritime Canada to be shipped all over the world. It only follows that we get to reap the rewards in our spectacular seafood markets and in our restaurants. We're lucky and we know it, but we also know that such bounty doesn't come without cost.

Fishing is a dangerous profession, and not just during the perfect storm. We're grateful to fishermen and their families, a key part of the rich fabric of New England, for bringing the best seafood in America to market. Their hard work makes it easy to put any of these wonderful recipes on the table whenever season and spirit move us.

"Eat fish and live longer," reads a sign at one Boston area sushi restaurant. I can't promise that, but I can point out that there are tremendous healthful benefits to making seafood part of your diet on a regular basis. So why wait? Go to the market, slip on your apron, and try one of these wonderful recipes for lunch or dinner.

Over the years, New England has convinced me there's nothing more satisfying than a simple shore supper, no matter where you enjoy it. That's not only how I became a seafood chef, it's why I'm a seafood fan.

Introduction

BY SHERYL JULIAN AND JULIE RIVEN

Like all New England cooks, we're both passionate and opinionated about seafood. Should chowder be white and creamy? Of course! We live in Boston and wouldn't have it any other way. Yet, when we head down to Rhode Island and we're offered their tomato-based version of the same dish, we're equally delighted.

New Englanders live surrounded by the sea — from Maine's rugged coastline to the sandy beaches of Connecticut. For centuries the ocean supplied what went onto supper tables all over this region. So we come by our seafood legacy out of practicality.

Some say New Englanders eat a lot of fish because tradition is strong here. But there's another, simpler reason: It's so good. Fish and potato chowders stirred over fireplaces centuries ago are still as popular as ever. Stop at any seafood market along the coast and you'll see tanks full of lobsters to buy and boil for dinner. And don't forget the steamers!

We're both professionally trained cooks, but our allegiance has always been to home cooks working hard to put healthy meals on the table. For more than 20 years in The Boston Globe Magazine, we've offered seafood classics — baked cod with buttery crumbs, fish and chips, warm potato salad to accompany a lobster meal — adding contemporary riffs here and there. We do tradition with a wink and a nod to stodgy old New England.

Lately, we've been turning tradition on its head, adding all kinds of nuances to our food. Now the crumbs on baked fish are often panko — the very crisp Japanese breadcrumbs that have become so popular. Fish isn't deep fried anymore (we leave that to restaurateurs like Jasper White), but rather "oven-fried" until crisp. Fish cakes, once made with salt cod, and later with boiled cod, are now shaped with uncooked fish, so the patties don't dry out in the skillet. And the old-fashioned Portuguese dish of steamers and sausages is made with turkey-based linguica or chorizo links. These adjustments have in mind your hearts, waistlines, and clocks.

In the following pages you'll find more classics and surprises culled from the Globe's Food section and Sunday Magazine, along with recipes from celebrity chefs. Some show off Maine's farmed mussels, serving them with a garlicky sauce or a spicy tomato mixture. Squid, another local favorite (a dish that's also deep-fried in restaurants and offered as calamari), is threaded onto skewers and grilled very quickly over hot coals. The mighty swordfish, cut into steaks, is also grilled and served with a tomato-olive salsa. And when skate wings come into the market, savvy shoppers rush home to slip them under the broiler, knowing that the flaky flesh is some of the most delectable seafood around.

That doesn't mean we don't all enjoy what our mothers cooked. The "Really Retro" dishes you'll find in these pages offer a throwback to an era that no one wants to forget. We still like to prepare baked shrimp covered with crushed, buttery Ritz crackers.

In summer and fall, Julie's husband fishes for blues and stripers. You won't eat better fish than striped bass that goes right from the boat to the kitchen. Bluefish with a mustard glaze is cooked over a wood-fueled fire, which makes the rich meat luxurious.

Our theory about seafood pretty much applies to all cooking. Recipes should be fresh tasting and made without fuss. Fish lends itself beautifully to the less-is-more rule. When company is coming, we head to the seafood market, ask the fishmonger what just arrived that day, and buy according to freshness. Guests are delighted and so are we. Dinner practically cooks itself.

shrimp boil

quick-fix crab cakes

oyster shooters

bay scallop ceviche

carpaccio of scallops

Appe

Here

Here in New England, where we've been known to pluck our hors d'oeuvres right from the sea, the nibbles that whet our appetites can be as simple as a beautifully shucked oyster topped by a tart mignonette; as traditional as a lightly fried cake of the freshest Maine crabmeat; or as exotic as a bay scallop ceviche, "cooked" in a little fresh lime juice. All are local. All are delicious. And, most important, all are easy enough for you to wow your family and friends, then relax and enjoy with them.

tizers

Our Favorite Little Fishing Shack ➤ BY STEVEN ROSENBERG, Globe Staff

You don't have to walk too far in Dock Square to find someone photographing, sketching, painting, or just staring at the red fishing shack that juts out into Rockport Harbor in coastal Massachusetts.

For artists, tourists, and business owners, there's an ineffable attraction to this reproduction of a simple wooden structure built to store fishing gear in the 1880s and named Motif #1 early last century by artist Lester Hornby, who recognized that it had become a standard subject for artists.

Since 1950, business owners have kicked off the tourist season every spring by celebrating Motif #1 Day. Most of the owners of the town's 49 galleries hold art demonstrations, and the musty red shack — built after the original one was blown down during the Blizzard of '78 — opens up to residents and tourists.

For the last 70 years, the shanty has been Rockport's postcard to the world. The exposure began when the US Navy anchored ships off Rockport's shore, with tourists embarking for tours on the ships from the shanty's granite wharf. In 1933, Rockport's business owners saw an opportunity to promote their town to middle America. That year, artists Aldro Hibbard and Anthony Thieme oversaw the design of a 27-foot replica of the motif, which was driven to the Chicago World's Fair. Along the way, 18 Rockport businessmen held tours of the float, illuminating the motif at night, as they passed out brochures describing their seaside town. In Chicago, it was entered into an American Legion parade with 200 other floats. The parade lasted 10 hours and passed by an estimated 2 million people. The motif won first prize and national acclaim, and returned to the cheers of 4,500 Cape Ann residents.

It's just as loved today.

Scallops are pulled up in a steel-framed drag, then cooked aboard the boat, using Captain Tom Bridges's special recipe.

Where Scallops Come From

 BY LETITIA BALDWIN, Globe Correspondent

An engine thrums and green and white lights glow in the harbor of Corea, Maine, a sleeping fishing village. Gray clouds of sea smoke envelop the broad-beamed wooden boat as it slips its mooring and steams out before dawn. Stars twinkle overhead and a rose-yellow band stretches across the eastern horizon as Tide & A Half's captain, Tom Bridges, heads for Gouldsboro Bay. There, he hoists a steel-framed drag, lowers it into the water, and starts fishing for scallops. Crew members Vivian Couture and Chuck Haycock hastily haul on orange waterproof overalls and insulated rubber gloves. Their breath fills the pilothouse.

Fifteen minutes later, Bridges raises the drag and swings it back on board. The steel-ringed bag opens and its contents cascade onto an ice-caked mat. The crew drop to their knees and begin picking sea scallops from the pile of kelp, seaweed, mussels, starfish, and rocks dragged up from the ocean floor. In frigid temperatures, Bridges and his crew will repeat this process at least a dozen times. Unlike larger scallop-

ers from New Bedford and Gloucester, who go fishing for 10 days or more at a time, Maine's scallop boats make day trips, and this extraordinarily fresh catch goes onto the tables of the best restaurants in the area.

In a primitive pantry, using small knives with curved blades and heavily taped handles, Couture and Haycock swiftly begin shucking, slitting open the shellfish, some encrusted with barnacles, and cut out the creamy white meat. Shells and guts are tossed overboard.

Tomorrow, perhaps, diners will savor scallop sashimi or pan-seared scallops artfully arranged with a vegetable puree and vinaigrette. And while restaurant-goers may pay dearly for those dishes, few realize the hazards and hardships involved in harvesting.

"Scalloping is one of the most dangerous fisheries because of the equipment. You are lifting it out of the water, with all that weight, over your head," Maine Marine Patrol lieutenant Alan Talbot says. "To me, everything is against [the scallopers]."

Castine Inn chef and owner Tom Gutow agrees. He's gone scalloping and learned how the shellfish is harvested. He buys all his scallops from local boats

The daily catch includes seaweed, mussels, and rocks dragged up from the ocean floor.

and serves them as ceviche, "cooked" in lime juice, garlic, and ginger. Or he might offer them as an entree with a cilantro vinaigrette and spicy celery root puree.

"Most people don't go to work with the prospect of risking their lives," notes Gutow, a volunteer fireman. "It is brutally cold, physically demanding, and almost mind-numbing work."

Bridges lobsters in spring, summer, and fall, and scallops all winter. On this day, the temperature never gets above 20 degrees, but the Corea

native is lightly clad in L. L. Bean boots, thin work pants, and a hooded sweatshirt.

Crew member Vivian Couture also seems in her element. She has raised two daughters, worked as a computer systems analyst, and dived for sea urchins. She earned a bachelor of science in molecular biology and biochemistry. This is her first season scalloping.

"I just wanted to do something different," Couture says. "This is a man's game. You have to be in tiptop shape. It's tough even for the guys."

Unlike clams or mussels, scallops can't hold their shells closed. That's why it's critical to shuck them quickly before they lose moisture and die.

Couture says it took her weeks to learn how to shuck, and she still doesn't feel quite up to speed. "Chuckie does two or three for my every one," says Couture, watching crewman Haycock shuck in one fast, fluid motion.

Late morning, Haycock fires up the propane stove and panfries scallops, barely cooking them. The golden nuggets have a sweet, nutty flavor and

taste like the ocean.

Bridges and his crew pause briefly, soaking up the sun and surveying the glittering sea. Snowcapped Cadillac Mountain rises in the distance. A raft of eider ducks shelters in the lee of a ledge.

This is what Bridges and other fishermen will tell you they treasure about their work despite its grueling, monotonous, and highly dangerous nature.

"It gets to be kind of a habit, you know what I mean?," he says. "You just got to love it."

Unlike clams or mussels, scallops can't hold their shells closed. That's why it's critical to shuck them quickly, before they lose moisture and die.

Carpaccio of Scallops
SERVES 2

Tom Gutow, of the Castine Inn, makes this with fine olive oil and Maine sea salt.

4 large sea scallops
Olive oil (for sprinkling)
Salt and white pepper, to taste
3 chives, finely chopped
1 small shallot, finely chopped

1. Remove the hinge from each scallop. Set the scallops on a large sheet of plastic wrap and pound them gently with the bottom of a small saucepan until they are as thin as possible without falling apart. Cover with another sheet of plastic wrap and refrigerate.
2. Remove the scallops from the refrigerator and carefully peel away the plastic wrap. Set each scallop on a chilled plate. Lightly brush each scallop with oil, then sprinkle them with salt and pepper. Drizzle lemon syrup around the scallops and sprinkle with chives and shallots.

LEMON SYRUP
1/4 cup water
1/4 cup sugar
Juice of 4 lemons
Pinch of ground turmeric

1. In a small saucepan, combine the water and sugar. Let the mixture cook over medium heat until the sugar dissolves. Bring to a boil and cook for 1 minute.
2. Pour the syrup into a bowl. Rinse the pan.
3. Pour the lemon juice into the pan with half the sugar syrup. Add more syrup to make a mixture that is a balance of sugar and acidity.
4. Add the turmeric and bring to a boil. Lower the heat and let the mixture cook to a thin syrup consistency. Set it aside to cool; it will thicken as it stands.
❧ LETITIA BALDWIN
adapted from the Castine Inn

Bay Scallop Ceviche
SERVES 4

The centuries-old method of "cooking" seafood by marinating it in citrus juice (and sometimes vinegar) is thought to be Peruvian. But Paul O'Connell, chef-owner of Chez Henri in Cambridge, Massachusetts, believes it probably originated on a beach in South America or the Caribbean, where fishermen would eat fresh catch sprinkled with the juice of native limes.

Besides scallops, other good choices for ceviche (also spelled seviche and pronounced sehVEEcheh or sehVEESH) are mahi mahi, red snapper, and tuna. You can use shellfish such as shrimp, lobster, or mussels, but you should cook them briefly first. Marinating times are up to the cook: 30 to 60 minutes will give you "rare" ceviche; three to four hours "cooks" the fish through.

Tiny bay scallops are the perfect size for ceviche. If you use the larger sea scallops, cut them into 1/2-inch dice or slice them crosswise.

12 ounces bay scallops, muscle removed, rinsed well in cold water, and drained
Juice of 3 limes
2 tablespoons chopped red onion
2 tablespoons chopped scallion (green part only)
1 tablespoon chopped jalapeño or other chili pepper
2 tablespoons finely chopped red bell pepper
1/4 to 1/2 cup lightly blanched corn kernels (when in season)
2 tablespoons chopped fresh cilantro
1 tablespoon olive oil
Sea salt and black pepper, to taste

1. In a mixing bowl, combine the scallops, lime juice, onion, scallion, chili pepper, bell pepper, corn, cilantro, and oil.
2. Cover with plastic wrap and refrigerate, stirring occasionally, for 1 1/2 to 2 hours. The scallops should be opaque on the outside, but they will be pink inside. (If you want fully "cooked" scallops, marinate them for 3 to 4 hours.)
3. Sprinkle with salt and pepper.
4. Divide the ceviche among 4 small bowls or stemmed glasses and serve chilled with crispy plantain chips.
❧ LISA ZWIRN
adapted from Chez Henri restaurant

Pick Your Crabmeat

🐟 BY LISA ZWIRN, Globe Correspondent

CRAB CAKE

True or false? Crabmeat you find at the supermarket or fish market is always cooked.

True. Surprisingly few people know that to "pick" a crab — that is, to remove the meat — it must first be cooked and shelled.

Unlike the lobster, which is prized alive, the crab, particularly in New England, is preferred picked, perhaps for the simple reason that the meat is hard to get to and there's not much of it. The only whole crabs (no longer kicking) typically found around here are soft shells, which are blue crabs that have molted and shed their hard shell.

Native rock and Jonah crabs are plucked out of the Atlantic from Massachusetts and Maine to Nova Scotia. They are less widely known than king and Dungeness crabs from the Pacific, blue crabs from the Chesapeake Bay, and Florida's renowned stone crabs. Offshore lobster fishermen catch most of our region's crabs as a byproduct of lobster fishing. (The same bait is used.)

Crabmeat is generally sold as "lump" (large pieces, mostly from the body), "jumbo lump" (even bigger pieces), and "flake" (small pieces), or labeled as claw or leg meat. The largest pieces picked from Maine crab, as much of the crabmeat sold around here is referred to, are from the legs and claws, whereas it's the body meat from blue crabs that is commonly sold as lump and jumbo lump because of the greater proportion of meat found on the blue crab's body.

New Englanders are partial to Maine crabmeat, and the reason may have something to do with pasteurization. Most native crabmeat isn't pasteurized, while blue crab, frequently sold canned in New England, is almost always heat-treated. Pasteurization, which is done to prolong shelf life, will rob crabmeat of some of its flavor.

So why is crabmeat always sold cooked? Think of it this way: Unlike fish, which are gutted to make them last longer, washed and iced on board the fishing boat, the hard shells encasing the meat of a crab or lobster make it impossible to gut and clean raw.

The lobster, which is worth far more whole and alive, is kept in saltwater tanks, while the crab is cooked quickly (lest it starts to decompose) and then picked for its tasty meat.

Quick-Fix Crab Cakes
MAKES 12

These crab cakes are delicious with red pepper jelly or chipotle mayonnaise for dipping.

1 pound fresh crabmeat,
*   picked over for shells*
1/2 cup finely chopped red bell pepper
1/3 to 1/2 cup fresh breadcrumbs
3 tablespoons chopped chives
1/4 cup mayonnaise
1 egg
1 tablespoon Dijon mustard
1 teaspoon Worcestershire sauce
1/2 teaspoon kosher salt
Black pepper to taste
4 tablespoons vegetable oil;
*   more as needed, for frying*
About 1/2 cup flour, for dredging

1. In a large bowl, place the crabmeat, bell pepper, 1/3 cup of the breadcrumbs, and chives.
2. In a measuring cup, mix together the mayonnaise, egg, Dijon mustard, Worcestershire sauce, and salt. Gently stir the mayonnaise mixture into the crabmeat. Season with pepper. Add more breadcrumbs if the mixture appears too thin. Refrigerate, covered with plastic wrap, until cooking time.
3. In a heavy, 12-inch skillet, heat the oil over medium heat. On a large plate, place the flour. Shape the crabmeat mixture into 12 cakes and coat them with flour. (The crab cakes will be soft, but will firm up as they cook.)
4. Set the oven at 250 degrees.

5. In a large skillet, heat 2 tablespoons of the oil. Add half of the fish cakes. Cook them, turning several times, for 10 to 12 minutes or until they are golden brown and cooked through.
6. Transfer the cooked patties to the warm oven. Use the remaining 2 tablespoons of oil to fry the remaining cakes in the same way.

CHIPOTLE MAYO
1/2 cup mayonnaise
1 chopped chipotle pepper (canned in
*   adobo sauce)*
Salt and black pepper, to taste

In small bowl, combine the mayonnaise with the chopped chipotle pepper. Add 1/2 to 1 teaspoon of adobo sauce, to taste, and season with salt and pepper.
— LISA ZWIRN

really retro

Crabmeat Dip
MAKES 1 CUP

Mixed with cream cheese and chopped pimento-stuffed olives, Maine crabmeat makes an old-fashioned dip – the kind served at a 1950s cocktail party.

1/2 large package cream cheese (4 ounces),
*   at room temperature*
1/2 red onion, finely chopped
1 tablespoon lemon rind
2 tablespoons lemon juice
2 tablespoons prepared white horseradish

2 tablespoons finely chopped
*   pimento-stuffed green olives*
6 ounces fresh crabmeat
Salt and pepper, to taste

1. In a bowl with a wooden spoon, work the cream cheese until it is soft and light. Stir in the onion, lemon rind, lemon juice, horseradish, and green olives.
2. When the mixture is smooth, add the crabmeat along with salt and pepper. Stir well. Taste for seasoning and add more horseradish if you like.
3. Cover with plastic wrap and refrigerate for up to 4 hours before serving with crackers or vegetables.
— SHERYL JULIAN AND JULIE RIVEN

Tartar Sauce
MAKES 1-2 CUPS

1/2 cup mayonnaise
1/2 cup plain (whole milk) yogurt
2 scallions, finely chopped
1/4 cup sweet pickle relish
2 tablespoons capers
2 tablespoons chopped fresh parsley
1 tablespoon Dijon mustard
1 tablespoon lemon juice
Salt and pepper, to taste
1 teaspoon water

1. In a bowl, combine the mayonnaise, yogurt, scallions, relish, capers, parsley, mustard, lemon juice, salt, and pepper.
2. Add the water and stir well. Cover tightly and refrigerate for 4 hours for the flavors to mellow before serving.
— SHERYL JULIAN AND JULIE RIVEN

Salmon Cakes
MAKES 8 CAKES

1 1/4-pound piece of boneless salmon
Vegetable oil (for drizzling and frying)
Salt and pepper, to taste
1 clove garlic, quartered
1/4 cup fresh dill leaves
20 plain crackers, such as saltines
1 egg
3 tablespoons bottled tomato-based
    cocktail sauce
Dash of Worcestershire sauce
Flour (for shaping)

1. Turn on the broiler. Set the salmon, skin side down, in an ovenproof baking dish and drizzle it lightly with oil, then sprinkle with salt and pepper. Broil the fish for 10 minutes or until it is cooked through. Set it aside to cool.
2. When the salmon is cool enough to handle, remove and discard the skin and any fatty pieces. In a bowl, flake the fish with a fork.
3. In a food processor fitted with the steel blade, work the garlic, dill, crackers, and salt and pepper until they are ground into crumbs. Add the cracker mixture to the fish with the egg, cocktail sauce, and Worcestershire sauce. Mix them until they are thoroughly blended.
3. Lightly flour the counter. Divide the salmon mixture into 8 pieces. With your hands, form the mixture into patties, coating them lightly with flour.
5. Set the oven at 250 degrees. In a large skillet, heat enough oil to make a thin film in the bottom of the pan. When it is hot, add half of the fish cakes. Cook them over medium-high heat, turning often, for about 10 minutes or until they are browned and cooked through. Transfer the cakes to the warm oven.
6. Use more oil to fry the remaining cakes in the same way. Serve at once with tartar sauce.

SHERYL JULIAN AND JULIE RIVEN
adapted from "The Way We Cook" (Houghton Mifflin)

White Fish Cakes
MAKES 12 CAKES

As it did a century ago, salt cod makes wonderful fish cakes. But the labor-intensive soaking process puts off modern cooks. Fresh cod was the fish of choice for so many decades that it became endangered, so cooks began to use pollock as an alternative. To ensure that the fish mixture has enough body to form a cake, work with it raw. Grinding uncooked fillets before adding them to mashed potatoes, keeps the fish from falling apart in cake form.

2 medium Idaho potatoes, peeled and cut
    into 1-inch pieces
1 cup whole milk
Salt and pepper, to taste
1 bunch scallions (white part only),
    cut into 1-inch pieces
1 small onion, quartered
1 pound skinless, boneless pollock fillets,
    cut into 2-inch chunks
1 egg
2 tablespoons chopped fresh lemon thyme
1/8 teaspoon cayenne pepper, or to taste
About 2 cups dry white breadcrumbs
    (for shaping)
4 tablespoons vegetable oil
3 tablespoons butter

1. In a saucepan, place the potatoes, milk, and a large pinch of salt. Add enough water to cover the potatoes completely.
2. Bring the water to a boil, lower the heat, and cook the potatoes for 20 minutes or until they are tender. Drain them and transfer them to a bowl. Mash them with a potato masher or a fork until they are smooth. Add plenty of pepper.
3. In a food processor fitted with the steel blade, work the scallions and onion until coarsely chopped. Add the uncooked pollock and process in on-off motions until the mixture is ground.
4. Stir the ground fish, egg, thyme, cayenne, salt, and pepper into the potatoes. Mix until well blended.
5. Sprinkle some of the breadcrumbs on the counter. Use a large metal serving spoon to take mounds of the fish and set them on the bread crumbs. Shape them into patties. (You should have 12.)
6. Set the oven at 250 degrees.
7. In a large skillet, heat 2 tablespoons of the oil. Add 1 1/2 tablespoons of the butter. When it melts, add half of the fish cakes. Cook them, turning several times, for 10 to 15 minutes or until they are golden brown and cooked through. (If the patties are thick, they may take longer; they should be opaque all the way through.)
8. Transfer the cooked patties to the warm oven. Use the remaining 2 tablespoons of oil and 1 1/2 tablespoons of butter to fry the remaining cakes in the same way. Serve at once with tartar sauce.

SHERYL JULIAN AND JULIE RIVEN

WHITE FISH CAKES

Smoked Bluefish Pate

SERVES 4

Bluefish, fishermen will tell you, is a fighting fish. It will bite your hand with smacking canine teeth that rattle when they go after prey. The meat is oily and soft and barely flakes. When smoked, it turns savory and smooth. The dark fish, however, is an acquired taste. In New England, where it is treasured, smoked bluefish was common long before smoker appliances became widespread.

Today, smoked bluefish is a small but steady commercial enterprise. New England smokehouses such as Fox Seafood of Narragansett, Rhode Island; Spence & Co. of Brockton, Massachusetts; and Sasquatch Smokehouse of Gloucester, Massachusetts include the rich fish in their product lines. For wholesale distribution, smoked blue fillets have to meet the Food and Drug Administration's salinity requirement (salt acts as a preservative).

Because the bluefish can be salty, add salt carefully in the recipe below, after the other ingredients have been mixed in. Dave Masch, who makes this creamy pate, writes a food column for On the Water magazine.

4 ounces boneless smoked bluefish
2 ounces cream cheese,
  at room temperature
1 tablespoon finely chopped onion
Dash of Worcestershire sauce
1 teaspoon lemon juice, or to taste
Salt and pepper, to taste

1. Remove the skin from the bluefish, if necessary. Break the fish into pieces. In a food processor, combine the bluefish and cream cheese. Pulse the mixture. Stop pulsing and remove the top. With a rubber spatula, scrape down the sides of the work bowl. Pulse again.
2. Add the onion, Worcestershire sauce, and lemon juice. Pulse several times. Taste for seasoning and add salt and pepper if you like. Pack the mixture into a bowl, smooth the top, and cover with plastic wrap.
3. Refrigerate for at least 1 hour and for as long as 3 days. Serve on crackers.

⅄ RACHEL ELLNER
adapted from Dave Masch

Steamers

SERVES 4

The clam broth in this recipe will be darker than you're used to because the onion and garlic are sautéed before the clams go into the pot.

24 soft-shelled clams
1 tablespoon ground black pepper
2 tablespoons olive oil
2 tablespoons chopped garlic
1 medium onion, chopped
1/4 teaspoon crushed red pepper
1 bottle (12 ounces) lager beer
1 1/2 cups water
1/2 cup (1 stick) unsalted butter, melted

1. Place the clams in a large bowl and add water to cover them by 2 inches. Add black pepper and gently swirl it into the water. Refrigerate the bowl for 20 minutes. This will clean out the clam bellies.

2. In a large skillet, heat the oil over high heat. Add garlic, onion, and crushed red pepper and cook for 5 minutes. Add the beer and water and bring to a boil. Add clams and cover tightly.
3. In a small skillet, melt the butter over low heat and set aside.
4. After the clams have cooked for 5 minutes, check them. As the clams open, use a slotted spoon to transfer them to a serving dish. The clams should all open in the next 2 minutes; discard any that do not open.
5. Line a strainer with several layers of cheesecloth and set it over a bowl. Strain the clam liquid through the cheesecloth and divide it among 4 small custard cups. (Refrigerate or freeze the remaining cooking liquid for a chowder.) Pour the melted butter into a small bowl or divide it among 4 small custard cups. Serve the clams at once, with clam broth and butter.

⅄ KERI FISHER

Stuffed Quahogs

SERVES 4

8 quahogs, scrubbed clean
2 strips bacon
1 tablespoon vegetable oil
1 medium onion, chopped
1 stalk celery, chopped
1 clove garlic, chopped
2 cups crumbled toasted bread
2 tablespoons fresh thyme, chopped
1/4 teaspoon cayenne pepper
Salt and pepper, to taste

1. Over a large bowl, shuck the quahogs, dropping the clams into

New England-isms

Up here — that's "heah" — in the coastal Northeast, people eat lobster and clams, which are pronounced "lobstah" and, uh, "clams." Following are a couple of items that are more likely to trip up non-natives in conversation.

QUAHOG A kind of hard-shelled clam, pronounced "co-hog." The verb form, "to quahog," suggests blocking access to something – as in, "At bar-mitzvah receptions and Greek and Italian wedding parties, some people quahog the buffet table."

SCROD Also spelled "schrod," but always pronounced "skrawd." The American Heritage Dictionary of the English Language defines it as "a young cod or haddock, especially one split and boned for cooking as catch of the day." Curiously, the dictionary says nothing about burying the fish under an inch of breadcrumbs, but that's what we like to do with it heah.

☛ ALAN LUPO AND OTHER GLOBE STAFF

the juice as they are opened. Reserve the shells. Gently swirl the clams in the juice to rinse them. Lift the clams out, chop them coarsely, and refrigerate them until ready to use.

2. Add enough water to the clam juice to increase the volume by half. Let it sit for about 5 minutes. Slowly pour off 2 cups of juice, leaving any sediment or sludge in the bowl. Discard the sediment and remaining juice.

3. Pick out eight of the nicest halfshells, scrub the inside clean, and set them aside to dry.

4. In a large skillet over medium heat, cook the bacon until it is crisp and golden. Remove it from the pan and transfer to paper towels.

5. Wipe out the pan. Add the oil, and when it is hot, cook the onion and celery for 8 minutes or until the onion softens. Add the garlic and clams and cook 2 minutes more.

6. Remove the pan from the heat. Stir in the crumbled toast, thyme, cayenne, salt, and pepper. Add enough of the reserved clam juice to make a mixture that holds together

and is slightly moist.

7. Divide the stuffing among the 8 shells, packing it in and mounding it slightly.

8. Turn on the broiler. Set the clams on a baking sheet. Slide the sheet under the broiler and cook the clams at least 8 inches from the element for 10 to 12 minutes or until they are browned. Watch them carefully so they do not burn. Serve at once.

❧ KERI FISHER

Steamed Mussels with Garlic

SERVES 4

Mussel cooking liquid makes an aromatic broth that you strain through cheesecloth and ladle over the mussels, with enough left to freeze for a chowder later.

2 tablespoons butter
1 Spanish onion, coarsely chopped
1 large carrot, coarsely chopped
1 stalk celery, coarsely chopped
1 1/2 cups dry white wine
3 thyme sprigs
Bunch of parsley stems
4 peppercorns
4 pounds mussels

1. In a large flameproof casserole, melt the butter and cook the onion, carrot, and celery over medium heat, stirring occasionally, for 10 minutes. Add the wine and bring to a boil. Turn the heat to medium and simmer for 5 minutes.

2. Tie the thyme, parsley, and peppercorns in cheesecloth and drop the bundle into the pot. Add the mussels, cover, and steam for 5 minutes or until they open. Use a slotted spoon to lift out and discard any unopened mussels.

3. Strain the broth. Reserve 2 cups for the mussel sauce and freeze the remainder for another use.

4. Place the mussels in a large bowl, cover with foil, and set aside.

SAUCE

2 tablespoons butter
2 cloves garlic, finely chopped
2 cups reserved broth
3 tablespoons chopped parsley
Salt and pepper, to taste

1. In a saucepan, melt the butter.

2. Add the garlic and cook, stirring, for 1 minute. Pour in the broth and bring to a boil.

3. Stir in the parsley, salt, and pepper.

4. Pour the sauce into four individual ramekins and serve immediately with the mussels.

❧ SHERYL JULIAN AND JULIE RIVEN

At the table, the mussels' blue-black shells are striking and festive. They seem dressy and fussed over. Discard any mussels that do not open after cooking.

STEAMED MUSSELS

How to Shuck an Oyster

The folks at B&G Oysters in Boston's South End shuck anywhere from 500 to 1,000 oysters every day. With that much practice, it's second nature to them. Chef Greg Reeves offers the following advice for do-it-yourselfers:

1. Rinse and scrub the oysters under cold water.
2. Hold the oyster against a counter or other flat surface with the cupped side down. Have a towel in the hand holding the oyster so you don't get cut by the ragged edges.
3. Insert the tip of an oyster knife into the hinge of the oyster as far as you can. When you feel the knife catch against the shell, twist it until the shell pops. Pull the knife out and clean it. You don't want any debris to contaminate the oyster.
4. Run the top of the knife along the top of the shell to loosen the large muscle. Remove the top shell.
5. Run the knife along the bottom shell to loosen the oyster from the shell.

☛ ANDREA PYENSON

Spicy Cocktail Sauce

MAKES 1 CUP

For a little extra zip, try serving this with your shucked oysters.

1/2 cup ketchup
Juice of 1 lemon
1/4 cup bottled white horseradish
1/2 teaspoon crushed red pepper (optional)
Dash of liquid hot sauce (optional)
Pinch of salt

In a bowl, combine the ketchup, lemon juice, horseradish, crushed pepper, hot sauce, and salt. Stir well.

☛ SHERYL JULIAN AND JULIE RIVEN

Oyster Shooters

SERVES 2

This recipe is a Bloody Mary takeoff that could hardly be sexier, or spicier. Be sure to get your oysters from a reputable fish monger, preferably on the day you plan to serve this, and store them, refrigerated, in their own juice. No matter what you have on the menu for later, once you've shot this back while staring into the eyes of the one you love or lust after, the night — if not the world — will surely be your oyster.

2 small, freshly shucked oysters
2 splashes ice cold vodka
  (plain, citrus, or jalapeño flavored)
2 teaspoons prepared cocktail sauce
2 teaspoons freshly grated horseradish
68 small capers
2 splashes Tabasco sauce
2 small stalks celery, with leaves,
  for garnish

1. Place each oyster in a shot glass.
2. To each glass, add a splash of vodka, 1 teaspoon cocktail sauce, 1 teaspoon horseradish, 34 capers, and a splash of Tabasco.
3. Garnish with celery. Make a toast and toss back.

☛ JOE YONAN
adapted from Ellen and Michael Albertson's "Temptations" (Fireside)

Be sure to get your oysters from a reputable fish monger and store them, refrigerated, in their own juice.

Shrimp Tales

Q What is the point of leaving the tail on shrimp?

ANSWER There are cosmetic and practical reasons to leave the tail on shrimp. With their tails intact, the shrimp look bigger. In a presentation, they look pretty, and they take up more room, which gives the impression of a greater volume of goodies. In a dish like shrimp cocktail, the last joint of shell and the fantail also make a decent handle. If you pinch the shell just above the tail, the last morsel of shrimp will pop out.

To remove the shell, hold the shrimp by the back, with the tail toward you, and grasp the little fins, or swimmerets (right below where the head used to be), with your other hand. With gentle but firm pressure, pull out and down. The shell, or exoskeleton, will begin to dismantle in obvious sections. To keep the tail on, stop peeling when there is one small layer of shell still encircling the tail. To remove the tail, grasp that bit of shell and pinch.

Whether you decide to leave the tail section on or not, run a small, sharp knife down the back of the shrimp to expose the vein, and rinse. When cooking shrimp at home, I peel the shrimp completely and use the shells for stock.

☞ PETER J. KELLY

Shrimp Cooked in Beer

SERVES 6

When an impromptu group gathers around someone's beach-house table, you can quickly cook shrimp in a beer bath and offer them in a big bowl along with a mayonnaise sauce mixed with French mustard, white wine vinegar, and lemon juice.

2 pints beer
2 pounds large shrimp, peeled
1 tablespoon Dijon mustard
1 tablespoon white wine vinegar
1 cup mayonnaise
2 tablespoons sour cream
Dash of Worcestershire sauce
Salt and pepper, to taste
Juice of 1/2 lemon
1 lemon, cut into 6 wedges
  (for garnish)

1. Using a large soup pot, empty the beer into the pot, then fill each empty bottle or can with water and tip the water into the pot. Add 2 more quarts of water. Bring to a boil.
2. Add the shrimp and cook for 2 to 3 minutes or until they turn pink and firm. Drain the shrimp into a colander and rinse with very cold water until they are no longer hot. Transfer them to a large bowl, cover with plastic wrap, and refrigerate until cold.
4. In a bowl, whisk together the mustard, vinegar, mayonnaise, and sour cream. Add the Worcestershire sauce, salt, and pepper. Stir thoroughly. Cover the bowl with plastic wrap and refrigerate until ready to use.
5. Sprinkle the shrimp with lemon juice, put the bowl in the center of the table, and serve with the mustard mayonnaise and lemon.

☞ SHERYL JULIAN AND JULIE RIVEN

GADGETS

Cutting Boards

A good cutting board is as indispensable to the well-thought-out kitchen as a sharp, high-quality knife. I'm a fan of wood, having been a long-time user of a **John Boos** (www.johnboos.com) board that is sturdy but still kind to my knife blades. But the Boos was scored with deep cuts, so I tested boards made from other materials to see if I should replace it.

I rejected a tempered glass model as being too hard on the knives, a bamboo version as too expensive for the small size, and disposable ones as environmentally unfriendly and fairly ridiculous.

Disposability isn't necessary to avoid cross-contamination, which occurs when bacteria from raw meat, poultry, or seafood comes in contact with vegetables, fruits, or other foods that don't get cooked to high enough temperatures to kill germs. The key is to clean boards properly (scrub with hot water and soap, then sanitize in the dishwasher or with a bleach solution), to sand out deep cuts in wood that might harbor germs, and, for extra safety, to use one cutting board for meat, poultry, or seafood, and another for everything else.

In the end, I settled on the **KatchAll Kolor-Cut Extra** (www.cooking.com), which is sold in color-coded sets to restaurants, but home cooks don't need all of them. I bought a green one to match my kitchen, and it has made the perfect companion to my beloved Boos board, which I spruced up with a good sanding and bleaching.

☛ JOE YONAN

Cassolette of Sea Urchin and Lobster SERVES 4

2 cups milk

1/2 pound parsnips, peeled and cut
    into 1/4-inch discs

2 tablespoons honey

3 ounces water

2 tablespoons lemon juice

1 pound butter (4 sticks),
    room temperature

Salt, to taste

1 cup sugar

1 cup water

Skin of 1 lemon

8 ounces sea urchin roe, cleaned

4 ounces cooked lobster meat, chopped

2 tablespoons sea beans,
    blanched and finely chopped

1 teaspoon jalapeño pepper,
    diced very small

1/2 teaspoon anchovy fillets,
    very finely chopped

Espelette pepper, to taste

Soy sauce, to taste

Lemon juice, to taste

Salt, to taste

Chives, chopped, for garnish

Korean long pepper threads, for garnish

Fried shallots, for garnish

Espelette pepper, for garnish

1. Make parsnip milk: In a small pot, combine the milk, parsnips, and honey, and bring to a simmer over medium heat. Allow the flavor to infuse in a warm place for two hours. Strain into a medium bowl and cool.

2. Make beurre monte: In a small saucepan, bring water and lemon juice to a boil. Remove from heat and slowly add butter, emulsifying with a hand blender. Season with salt and reserve in a warm place.

3. Make preserved lemon: In a small saucepan, combine sugar and water and bring to a boil. Turn heat to low, add lemon skin, and cook slowly until lemon is semitransparent, about 10 minutes.

4. In a medium-size pot over very gentle heat, combine 6 ounces of beurre monte and 3 ounces parsnip milk. Add sea urchin roe, lobster meat, sea beans, jalapeño, and anchovy. Season with espelette, soy sauce, lemon juice, and salt.

5. In a separate pot, heat the parsnip milk over low heat. When it is warm, turn the heat off and foam the milk using an immersion blender.

6. Thinly slice 1 teaspoon of preserved lemon and divide equally among 4 serving bowls.

7. Once the urchin and lobster mixture is warm, divide it equally among the bowls. Top it with the parsnip milk foam, and garnish with chives, Korean long pepper threads, fried shallots, and espelette.

 KEN ORINGER

KEN ORINGER
After working in some of America's top kitchens, this New Jersey native settled in Boston, where he opened Clio in 1997. His creativity earned him the James Beard Best Chef/ Northeast award (2001) and more acclaim for his Uni sashimi bar and tapas-inclined Toro. He also made People magazine's "Top 50 Bachelors" list in 2002, but that's a whole other story.

"Sea beans and sea urchin roe are worth seeking out. Trust me; they're no scarier than a raw oyster."

shrimp tabbouleh

grilled squid

lobster vinaigrette on a bed of green

crabmeat-filled avocado

smoked bluefish

Salads

Once

upon a time, seafood salad almost always meant lobster or crabmeat mixed with mayonnaise and, depending on your taste, diced celery. Not that there was anything wrong with that. There will always be a place for traditional seafood salads. But times have changed. Tastes have evolved. Today the seafood in salads comes poached, steamed, smoked, or grilled, served hot or cold, with or without shells. The salads can be as complex as Israeli couscous with tuna, chickpeas, green beans, red peppers, and cherry tomatoes, or as simple as grilled squid with fresh herbs, lemon juice, and olive oil. Really, the possibilities are as vast as the sea.

CRABMEAT SALAD

GRILLED SQUID SALAD

Seafood Salad Moves Beyond Mayo

⌖ BY SARAH TOMLINSON, Globe Correspondent

Seafood salad is cosmopolitan these days, according to Roger Berkowitz, owner and chief executive officer of Legal Sea Foods. Sure, mayonnaise-drenched lobster or crab is an oldie-but-goodie that can still be jazzed up, but seafood now steps out with international grains, such as bulgur and couscous, as well as fresh herbs, vinaigrettes, and curry. It's just a matter of preparing and dressing the seafood.

No matter what flavors Berkowitz uses for his seafood salads, fish is usually poached. Place a meat rack in a pan filled with salted water to just above the rack. Heat water, add the fish, and gently boil for about 10 minutes per pound. Undercook the fish slightly, remove from the heat, and cool in the poaching liquid.

Other ingredients can be added to the water to impart flavor, including: fish broth made from fish bones boiled down in water; garlic, salt, and pepper; wine and a few carrots; lemon zest, salt, and pepper; celery, fresh herb stems, and a lemon wedge.

Fish also can be seasoned directly. Rub soy sauce on salmon before poaching, or sprinkle garlic on the flesh of any fish.

Clams and mussels can be steamed in a half-cup of white wine or other liquid per pound. Stir several times and cook until the shells open.

Poach shrimp in a mixture of wine, bay leaves, lemon, and peppercorns that have been simmered together. Add the shrimp, cover with liquid, and simmer for about five minutes until shells turn pink.

Grill seafood after it has been marinated in vinaigrette.

Use smoked mussels or salmon, instead of fresh, to add flavor.

Salmon goes well with dill or herbs that have small, light leaves, such as chervil, tarragon, chives, and cilantro.

Salt is often enough for truly fresh seafood. "When you get really fresh seafood, you don't need to cover it up with sauces," says Berkowitz.

Grilled Shrimp and Arugula Caesar

SERVES 4

Contemporary Caesars use the nicest lettuces in the market and some aromatic olive oil, but the rest is up to the cook. Some inventions, such as grilled shrimp and arugula Caesar with corn-muffin croutons, are only vaguely related to the original. But who cares, when we've come to praise Caesar?

1 pound large shrimp, peeled
2 tablespoons olive oil
Juice of 1 lime
2 tablespoons fresh thyme leaves
Salt and pepper, to taste
4 store-bought corn muffins, cut into 1/2-inch rounds
1 tablespoon vegetable oil
2 bunches arugula, rinsed, dried, and stemmed
Caesar dressing without egg (see recipe)
1/2 cup grated Romano cheese

1. In a large bowl, toss together the shrimp, oil, lime juice, thyme, salt, and pepper. Cover and refrigerate for 1 hour.
2. Brush the rounds of corn muffin with vegetable oil.
3. Prepare a gas or charcoal grill. When it is hot, carefully grill the shrimp and corn muffins, turning them often. Cook the shrimp for 2 minutes on each side or until they are bright pink and cooked through. The corn muffins should be lightly toasted.
4. Arrange the muffin rounds overlapping on each of 4 dinner plates. Divide the shrimp among the plates. Toss the arugula with dressing and top each plate with some of the greens. Add salt, pepper, and Romano cheese. Serve at once.

❧ SHERYL JULIAN AND JULIE RIVEN

Caesar Dressing

MAKES 1 CUP

1 clove garlic, coarsely chopped
4 anchovy fillets, cut up
Dash of Worcestershire sauce
Juice of 1 lemon
1 tablespoon Dijon mustard
Salt and pepper, to taste
1/2 cup Parmesan cheese
1/2 cup olive oil

1. In the bowl of a food processor, combine the garlic, anchovies, Worcestershire sauce, lemon juice, and mustard. Pulse until the mixture is thoroughly combined. Add salt, pepper, and cheese and mix until smooth.
2. With the machine running, add the oil through the feed tube 1/2 teaspoon at a time until the dressing emulsifies. Taste for seasoning, add more salt and pepper, if necessary.

❧ SHERYL JULIAN AND JULIE RIVEN

Shrimp Tabbouleh

SERVES 4

1 cup bulgur
1 sweet onion, chopped
5 ripe tomatoes, chopped
1 large cucumber, chopped
1/2 cup fresh mint, finely chopped
1/4 cup fresh parsley, finely chopped
1/4 cup lemon juice
1 teaspoon lemon zest (optional)
1/3 to 1/2 cup olive oil
Freshly ground black pepper
1 pound cooked shrimp, shelled, or whole cooked mussels
Salt (optional)
Mint leaves for garnish

1. Cover the bulgur with water and let stand for at least one hour, until it has softened. The grains will swell, so add more water when necessary.
2. When the bulgur is soft, yet chewy, drain and place in a clean dish towel to squeeze it dry.
3. Place the bulgur in a non-reactive bowl and add onion, tomatoes, cucumber, mint, parsley, lemon juice, lemon zest (if using), oil, and pepper.
4. Just before serving, add the shrimp or mussels. Add salt to taste, if desired. Garnish with mint leaves.

❧ SARAH TOMLINSON
adapted from Roger Berkowitz and Jane Doerfer's "The New Legal Sea Foods Cookbook" (Broadway Books)

Add a new dimension to any salad by dressing up the greens with marinated and cooked shrimp.

CHIRASHI-ZUSHI

Chirashi-zushi, or scattered sushi, is rice spread in a box or bowl with fish and vegetables scattered on top or mixed in.

Shrimp Ceviche

SERVES 4

The South American dish ceviche is made with raw fish or shellfish that is "cooked" in citrus juices with herbs and hot chilies. In this recipe, which uses jicama to make a crunchy salad, the shrimp are first soaked briefly in salted water, then cooked for 1 minute before being added to the marinade. This allows you to serve the dish within 2 hours.

1 1/2 pounds large unshelled shrimp,
  thawed and soaked in cold salted water
  for 20 minutes
Juice of 4 limes
1/3 cup olive oil
Salt and pepper, to taste
1/4 cup fresh cilantro leaves,
  finely chopped
1/4 red onion, finely chopped
1 yellow bell pepper, cored, seeded,
  and finely chopped
1 poblano chili pepper, cored, seeded,
  and finely chopped
1 medium jicama, peeled and
  cut into thin matchsticks
4 scallions, sliced diagonally,
  1/4-inch wide
1 extra lime, cut into wedges (for garnish)

1. Have on hand a large bowl of ice water. Bring a large pot of water to a brisk boil. Add the shrimp and cook for 1 minute exactly (they will not be cooked through). Drain in a colander and plunge them into ice water. When the shrimp are cold, drain and peel them.

2. Transfer the shrimp to a bowl. Add the lime juice, oil, salt, pepper, cilantro, red onion, half of the bell pepper, and the poblano pepper. Stir gently but thoroughly.

3. Cover with plastic wrap and refrigerate for 2 hours, or until the shrimp are no longer raw — or up to 8 hours.

4. To serve, arrange the jicama on 4 salad plates, spoon the shrimp and vegetables on top, and garnish with the remaining bell pepper, scallions, and lime wedges.

❦ SHERYL JULIAN AND JULIE RIVEN

Cellophane Noodle Salad with Shrimp and Salmon

SERVES 4

From Sri Owen's very good book, "Noodles the New Way," comes this Thai shrimp and salmon salad with cellophane noodles. Owen says that there are many spicy fish salads in Thailand. She toned this version way down, she writes. Serve it with a little Thai chili sauce. Cellophane noodles, also called bean threads or mung bean sticks, are fully cooked and only need soaking. If you want to prepare the noodles several hours in advance, leave them in cold water to prevent them from sticking together.

3 1/2 ounces cellophane noodles
Salt, to taste
16 very small button mushrooms
1/2 English cucumber,
  halved lengthwise and seeded
1/4 cup lemon juice
2 teaspoons sugar
1 teaspoon salt
1 tablespoon light soy sauce
1 bird's-eye chili pepper,
  very finely chopped, or a large pinch
  of cayenne pepper
1 small shallot, thinly sliced
1 tablespoon chopped scallion
1 tablespoon chopped cilantro leaves
16 extra-large shrimp, cooked
4 ounces smoked salmon,
  cut into julienne strips
2 heads Belgian endive, pulled apart
  into leaves (for serving)

1. Bring a kettle of water to a boil. Turn it off and let it stand for 5 minutes. Put the noodles into a large bowl and add enough hot water to cover them completely. Let them sit for 5 minutes. Drain them, rinse them with cold water until they are cool, and drain them again.

2. In a small saucepan filled with salted water, bring the mushrooms to a boil. Cook them for 2 minutes, then drain them.

3. Slice the cucumber thinly. Transfer it to a bowl. Add the lemon juice, sugar, salt, soy sauce, chili pepper or cayenne, shallot, scallion, and cilantro. Stir to dissolve the sugar and salt. Add the mushrooms, shrimp, and smoked salmon.

4. Use scissors to snip the noodles several times so they are easy to eat.

5. Arrange the endive on each of 4 dinner plates. Divide the noodles among the plates, and top with the shrimp and cucumber mixture. Serve at once.

❦ SHERYL JULIAN AND JULIE RIVEN
adapted from Sri Owen's "Noodles the New Way" (Villard)

Chirashi-zushi

SERVES 4

Make this "salad" of vegetables and fish with seasoned rice when you need a picnic or summer supper dish. Use cooked or smoked fish. Save raw fish for a time when you're not transporting food.

2 eggs, lightly beaten
1 tablespoon sugar
1/2 teaspoon salt
1/2 teaspoon vegetable oil
5 cups cooked sushi rice
  (see recipe in Pasta &Rice chapter)
1/2 pound cooked shrimp
1 1/2 cups frozen green peas, thawed
1/2 pound smoked salmon,
  cut into matchsticks
1 pickling cucumber, peeled, seeded,
  and chopped
1 cup snow peas,
  blanched and thinly sliced
Seasoned shiitake mushrooms
  (see recipe)
2 tablespoons shredded red pickled ginger

1. In a bowl, stir the eggs, sugar, and salt together. Rub the bottom of a 6-inch nonstick skillet with a drop of oil.
2. Add one-quarter of the egg mixture. Swirl it around to spread into a thin crepe. Cook 1 minute or just until bubbles appear. With a metal palette knife, turn the crepe over and cook 30 seconds more. Turn out onto a plate. Fry 3 more crepes. Cut them into fine strips.
3. Place the sushi rice in large bowl. Scatter three-quarters of the shrimp, green peas, salmon, cucumber, snow peas, and shiitakes on top of the rice. Garnish with egg strips, remaining shrimp and ginger.

SEASONED SHIITAKE MUSHROOMS

8 dried shiitake mushrooms
3/4 cup mushroom soaking liquid
3 tablespoons soy sauce
2 tablespoons sugar
1 tablespoon Mirin (sweet rice wine)

1. In a bowl, combine the mushrooms and enough hot water to cover them. Soak for 30 minutes. Lift out the mushrooms (reserve the liquid) and rinse them. Cut them into strips.
2. In a saucepan, combine the mushrooms, 3/4 cup of the mushroom liquid, soy sauce, sugar, and Mirin. Bring to a boil, lower the heat, and simmer for 5 minutes or until the mushrooms have almost absorbed the liquid.
☙ DEBRA SAMUELS

Smoked Bluefish Salad

SERVES 4

Serve this rich salad over lettuce greens, with crackers, or stuffed into a crusty baguette.

1/2 pound smoked bluefish
1/2 cup finely chopped celery
2 tablespoons chopped red onion
1 tablespoon coarsely chopped capers
  (optional)
2 tablespoons chopped Italian parsley
1 tablespoon red wine vinegar
1 tablespoon lemon juice
2 tablespoons mayonnaise, or more to taste
Pepper, to taste

1. If necessary, remove the skin and bones from the bluefish. With your hands, pull it apart into large flakes. Transfer to a bowl.
2. Add the celery, onion, capers (if using), parsley, vinegar, lemon juice, mayonnaise, and pepper. Fold gently, taste for seasoning, and add more mayonnaise or pepper, if you like.
☙ RACHEL ELLNER
adapted from Bob Rakovic of Fox Seafood in Rhode Island

John D. Rockefeller and cookbook maven Fannie Farmer made lobster consumption more popular in the United States. Rockefeller, who summered in Maine, was served lobster stew by mistake (it was meant for his servants) and ordered it regularly thereafter.

Grilled Squid Salad

SERVES 4

You have to be confident to grill seafood. It cooks in so little time that it can change from beautifully done to overcooked in the minute it takes to step away from the grill to replenish your wine glass. Hover over freshly caught fish.

10-inch wooden skewers
1 pound young squid
Olive oil (for brushing)
Salt and pepper, to taste
1 small red onion, halved and thinly sliced
1 English cucumber, thinly sliced
3 tablespoons chopped fresh parsley
2 tablespoons lemon juice
2 tablespoons olive oil

1. Soak the skewers in water for 1 hour. Using kitchen shears, cut open the squid bodies so each can be flattened into a triangle shape. Halve each one lengthwise into 2 smaller triangles.
2. Weave the skewers through the flesh and the tentacles, so the pieces of squid will lie flat during grilling. Brush both sides of the squid with oil and sprinkle with salt and pepper. Refrigerate for 20 minutes.
3. Prepare a gas or charcoal grill. Brush the rack with oil. When grill is hot, set the squid on the rack and cook for 1 minute. Turn the squid and cook for 30 seconds more. The squid will change from opaque to white very quickly. As soon as it turns white, it is done. If the flesh overcooks, it toughens. Transfer the squid to a platter.
4. In a bowl, toss the onion, cucumber, salt, pepper, and parsley. Remove the squid from the skewers and add it to the bowl. Toss gently.
5. In a small bowl, whisk the lemon juice and 2 tablespoons of oil together. Sprinkle the salad with the dressing, toss gently again, and serve at once.

⏰ SHERYL JULIAN AND JULIE RIVEN

Crabmeat-Filled Avocado

SERVES 4

Mix sweet Maine crabmeat with a few crunchy vegetables and a couple of spoonfuls of mayonnaise and serve it on a ripe avocado half or inside a scooped-out tomato. That's so retro, you'll have to pass Melba toast.

2 ripe avocados
Juice of 1 lemon
6 ounces fresh crabmeat
2 stalks celery, finely chopped
4 scallions, finely chopped
1/2 red bell pepper, cored, seeded, and finely chopped
2 tablespoons finely chopped parsley
6 tablespoons mayonnaise
3 tablespoons lime juice
Salt and black pepper, to taste

1. With a paring knife, halve the avocados. Use the tip of the knife to pierce the pits and lift them out of the avocados. Use a serving spoon the same size as the avocado half to scoop the flesh from the skin. Discard the skin. Sprinkle the avocados all over with lemon juice.
2. In a bowl, combine the crabmeat, celery, scallions, red pepper, parsley, 4 tablespoons of the mayonnaise, 2 tablespoons of the lime juice, salt, and black pepper. Stir well.
3. Set an avocado half, cut side up, on each of 4 salad plates. Divide the crabmeat mixture among the avocados.
4. In a bowl, stir the remaining 2 tablespoons of mayonnaise until it is light. Add the remaining 1 tablespoon of lime juice. Spoon the mayonnaise over the crabmeat salad and serve at once.

⏰ SHERYL JULIAN AND JULIE RIVEN

Crab and Pea Tendril Salad

SERVES 4

Chef Andy Husbands of Boston's Tremont 647 restaurant says this dish would go well with freshly grilled bread and a glass of Billecart-Salmon Brut Champagne.

1/4 cup butter
1 tablespoon extra-virgin olive oil
4 garlic cloves, minced
1 bottle Champagne
2 lemons, quartered and seeded
2 teaspoons fresh thyme leaves
1 tablespoon Old Bay seasoning
1 cup fresh peekytoe or Dungeness crabmeat
1 cup roasted red peppers, julienned
1/2 red onion, julienned

Salt and freshly cracked
  black pepper to taste
1/2 pound pea tendrils

1. In a heavy pan, place the butter,
oil, and garlic over high heat. Sauté,
stirring frequently, until the garlic
and butter start to brown.
2. Add the Champagne and lower
the heat to medium. Let the
Champagne reduce by two-thirds
(about 4 to 6 minutes), then remove
from the heat.
3. Squeeze the lemon quarters and
add them, along with the thyme,
Old Bay seasoning, crabmeat, red
peppers, and onion. Season with salt
and pepper, then toss with the pea
tendrils and serve immediately.
▼ JOE YONAN
adapted from Andy Husbands

Mussel Salad
Ⓢ Ⓔ Ⓡ Ⓥ Ⓔ Ⓢ ④

1 recipe Steamed Mussels with Garlic
  (see Appetizers chapter), shell all mussels
  but do not make sauce
1 red bell pepper, cored, seeded,
  and chopped
1/2 red onion, thinly sliced
2 tablespoons chopped fresh parsley
1 tablespoon olive oil
2 tablespoons red wine vinegar

Salt and black pepper, to taste
Boston lettuce (for serving)

1. In a bowl, combine the mussels,
red pepper, onion, and parsley. Toss
well. Sprinkle the oil and vinegar on
the mussels, add salt and pepper, and
toss again.
2. Plate the mussels on lettuce. Serve
with toasted pita bread.
▼ SHERYL JULIAN AND JULIE RIVEN

Lobster Vinaigrette on a Bed of Greens
Ⓢ Ⓔ Ⓡ Ⓥ Ⓔ Ⓢ ④

You can serve the lobster halves in
or out of their shells for this salad,
or buy cooked lobster meat at a good
fish market (you'll need 8 ounces).
Any greens can form the cushion.
Here, lettuce, watercress, endive,
and cherry tomatoes are used.

2 whole lobsters, cooked
12 leaves of red-leaf, romaine, or
  leaf lettuce
1 bunch watercress
2 heads Belgian endive
1 pint yellow or red cherry tomatoes

Handful fresh chives,
  snipped into 1-inch pieces
3 tablespoons white wine vinegar
1 teaspoon grainy French mustard
1 clove garlic, crushed
Salt and freshly ground black pepper,
  to taste
1/4 cup olive oil

1. Halve the lobsters lengthwise
and remove the tail, claws, and
"swimmerets" (the tiny feelers)
from the body.
2. Cut up the lettuce leaves and
arrange some on each of four
dinner plates. Cut the watercress
sprigs from the stems and scatter the sprigs on the lettuce. Pull
off the endive leaves and arrange
them on the plates. Halve or
quarter the cherry tomatoes and
scatter them on the plates with
the chives.
3. Put the tail, claws, and swimmerets from half a lobster on each
of the salads.
4. In a small bowl whisk together
the vinegar, mustard, garlic, salt,
and pepper. Whisk in the oil a
little at a time until the dressing
emulsifies. Taste for seasoning and
sprinkle some dressing on each
plate. Serve at once.
▼ SHERYL JULIAN AND JULIE RIVEN

Whether preparing wild or cultivated mussels, remove
each mussel beard. Grab the beard with your fingertips and
pull it away from the hinge. This should snap off the beard,
along with its root, so that no part of the beard is left.

SHRIMP CEVICHE

Juicers

T When a seafood dish requires citrus juice, a tool comes in handy if you want to get more than a couple of tablespoons. The old standby is a reamer, usually made of plastic or wood. You hold the halved lemon in one hand and the reamer in the other, and you squeeze, twist, ram and ream, hopefully working over a bowl, then strain out all the pulp and seeds. The control lets you get every last bit of juice from a citrus fruit, but the going is slow and painful if you have exposed cuts on your fingers.

There are other ways to get juice. **Oxo** (www.oxo.com) has a juicer in its Good Grips line built on a measuring cup base. It includes a strainer and two-sided reamer that you flip over for larger or smaller fruit, and, as usual, a comfortable grip on one side. It is especially good for relatively small jobs, such as juicing enough to make ceviche.

Consider **KitchenAid** (www. kitchenaid.com), whose stand mixers are must-have equipment for home bakers, has adapted a Mexican design for a hand juicer that is shaped like a giant garlic press. You put a lime, lemon, or orange half (cut side down) on one side, then close the other side around it, press, and juice comes through the holes.

If you don't mind giving up some counter space, and your juicing needs involve drink-making more often than seasoning, consider a full-fledged appliance. An electric juicer by **Cuisinart** (www.cuisinart.com) consistently extracted the most juice in the least amount of time when I tested it. But speed isn't everything. For comfort and looks, the **OrangeX** Ojex juicer (www.orangex.com), a standing cast-iron press, is a keeper. It's harder to clean than the others, but otherwise so easy to use that it may tempt you to throw a margarita party.

☞ JOE YONAN

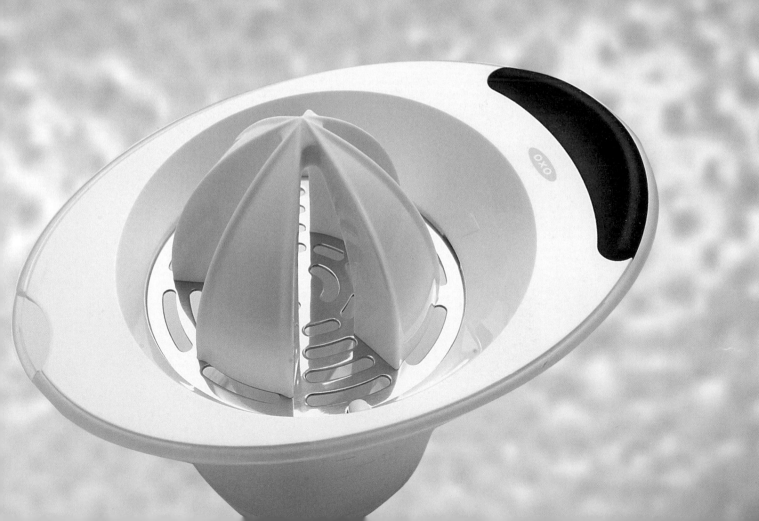

Tuna, Bean, and Cornichon Salad

SERVES 2

Large flakes of Italian tuna in olive oil make this simple salad, with green beans, cherry tomatoes, and tiny French cornichon pickles, a memorable dish. The tuna is available at specialty markets and in many North End groceries. Our favorite brand is Flott.

1/2 pound green beans, trimmed
1/2 pint cherry tomatoes, halved
1/2 poblano pepper, cored, seeded, and thinly sliced
1/4 cup chopped black olives
1 cup canned chickpeas
1 jar or can (7 1/2 ounces) Italian tuna in olive oil
1/4 cup thinly sliced cornichons
1/4 cup chopped fresh parsley
Salt and pepper, to taste
1 teaspoon grainy French mustard
1/4 cup white wine vinegar
1/3 cup olive oil

1. Bring a saucepan of water to a boil. Have on hand a bowl of ice water. Add the beans and blanch them for 2 minutes. Drain the beans into a colander and then quickly transfer them to the ice water. When the beans are cold, drain them again and pat them dry with paper towels.

2. Cut the beans in half and transfer to a mixing bowl. Add the tomatoes, poblano pepper, olives, and chickpeas. With a fork, flake the tuna into large pieces. Add the tuna, pickles, and parsley to the bowl. Toss gently to mix.

3. In a small bowl, whisk together the salt, black pepper, mustard, and vinegar. Gradually whisk in the oil until it is all added.

4. Add 2 tablespoons of the dressing to the salad and toss. Continue adding dressing, 1 tablespoon at a time, until the tuna and vegetables are coated. Refrigerate any unused dressing.

⌣ SHERYL JULIAN AND JULIE RIVEN

Israeli Couscous Salad with Chickpeas and Tuna

SERVES 8

Couscous is the new rice. The tiny grains of semolina that are served with Morocco's famous national dish are appearing in all kinds of other recipes. The granular pasta has a distinct advantage over its competitors: It requires hardly any cooking. Israeli couscous (also called Middle Eastern) cooks in 8 minutes. The tiny balls make an unusual presentation in this salad with chickpeas and canned tuna.

2 cups Israeli couscous, available at specialty markets
Salt and black pepper, to taste
Olive oil (for sprinkling)
1 pound green beans, trimmed and cut into thirds
1 can (15 ounces) chickpeas
2 cans or jars (6 to 8 ounces each) tuna in oil
1/2 cup pitted black olives
1/4 cup chopped fresh parsley
1 bunch scallions, finely chopped
1 red bell pepper, cored, seeded, and finely chopped
1 pint cherry tomatoes, halved
Juice of 1 lemon, or to taste
2 tablespoons olive oil (optional)

1. Bring 2 quarts of water to a boil. Add the couscous and a generous pinch of salt. When the water returns to a boil, cook the couscous for 8 minutes or until it is tender but still has a little bite.

2. Drain the couscous in a colander. Sprinkle with a little olive oil and toss to coat. Transfer to a large mixing bowl.

3. In a saucepan fitted with a steamer insert, steam the green beans over several inches of boiling water, covered, for 3 to 5 minutes or until they are tender but still have some bite. Rinse them with very cold water until they are no longer hot. Set them on paper towels to dry.

4. Drain the chickpeas in a colander, then rinse them, shaking the colander to remove the excess water.

5. Drain and flake the tuna, reserving the oil.

6. Add the chickpeas to the couscous with the olives, parsley, scallions, bell pepper, tomatoes, tuna, and green beans.

7. Toss gently. Add enough of the reserved tuna oil to lightly coat the salad.

8. Add the lemon juice a little at a time until it balances the oil. Taste for seasoning and add more salt, pepper, and the remaining olive oil if you like.

⌣ SHERYL JULIAN AND JULIE RIVEN

A veteran clam
digger works
a flat in the
Germantown
section of
Quincy,
Massachusetts,
at sunrise.

Spicy Sicilian Bread Salad with Marinated Tuna

SERVES 8

4 yellowfin tuna fillets (2 pounds),
  without the skin
Salt and pepper, to taste
1 1/2 cups extra virgin olive oil
1 fennel bulb, outer leaves
  and core removed, finely chopped
2 cloves garlic, minced
1/2 cup mint leaves, roughly chopped
1 cup pitted green olives, such as Picholine,
  roughly chopped
Juice of 1 lemon
8 cups of peasant-style Italian bread,
  torn into 1/4-inch pieces
8 ripe tomatoes, peeled and finely chopped
12 scallions, white part only, chopped
1 tablespoon capers, rinsed
1/2 cup chopped French cornichons
2 pepperoncini, chopped
2 teaspoons dried Greek oregano
4 tablespoons fresh parsley, chopped

1. Sprinkle each side of the tuna with salt and pepper.

2. In a sauté pan large enough to hold the 4 fillets, heat 2 tablespoons of olive oil over medium-high heat. Add the tuna fillets and lightly brown one side, about 4 minutes. Turn the fish over and brown the other side, about 4 minutes (depending on the thickness of the tuna). The tuna should be just cooked through with a little pink left in the center. Remove the tuna from the pan and set on a baking sheet or large tray to cool for about 10 minutes.

3. When the tuna is cool enough to handle, break it into 1/2-inch to 1/4-inch chunks and place it into a large mixing bowl, with any juices or oils that gathered while it was resting. Stir in finely chopped fennel, garlic, mint, and olives. Re-season with salt and pepper to taste, adding the juice of 1/2 lemon. Allow to marinate for at least one hour in the refrigerator before serving.

4. Set the oven at 300 degrees. Spread the bread on a baking sheet and bake until lightly toasted, about 8 minutes.

5. Place the bread in a large mixing bowl. Stir in the tomatoes, 1 cup of olive oil, scallions, capers, cornichons, pepperoncini, oregano, parsley, and remaining lemon juice. Season with salt and pepper to taste. Allow to sit for 20 minutes.

6. Serve side by side with the marinated tuna or mix the tuna into the bread salad and serve as one salad.

❦ ANA SORTUN

ANA SORTUN
A native of Seattle, Sortun made a splash in New England by blending French technique and training with Mediterranean flavors and ingredients. She opened Oleana in Cambridge, Massachusets, in 2001, and was named 2005 Best Chef/Northeast by the James Beard Foundation. Her first cookbook is "Spice: Flavors of the Eastern Mediterranean" (Regan Books).

"This is not any ordinary tuna salad. It transports me to the Mediterranean."

oyster stew

Greek fish soup

skate chowder

New England fish chowder

lobster stew

Soups

We're pretty open-minded in New England. If some people want to think that a soup of clams in red broth is clam chowder, we'll let them. We know the truth ...We also know that if you steam, simmer, or boil just about anything that once lived in the waters off our shores in a rich broth, toss in some vegetables and spices, and maybe add some milk or cream (if you're really thinking chowder) there is no end to the delights you can create — hearty one-dish meals, or simple first courses in a bowl. Perfect any time of year, whatever you call them.

AND Stews

Oysters: The Toast of Cape Cod

 BY ANDREA PYENSON, Globe Correspondent

The more you talk to oyster connoisseurs, the more you hear the language of wine experts. They refer to an oyster's "finish" and describe the taste as "crisp," "clean," or "fruity" with "vegetable overtones."

Nowhere is the taste and texture of the oyster examined more closely than on Cape Cod, described as the Napa Valley of shellfish by fisheries and aquaculture specialist Bill Walton. Oysters grown in cold, clear water — as on the Cape or in Canada — have a sweetness to them, says Walton, who works at the Cape Cod Cooperative Extension.

Even within the Cape, conditions, and therefore flavor, vary from bay to bay and grower to grower.

The analogy to wine is apt. The environment in which oysters grow has everything to do with how they taste, much as the characteristics of wine are largely determined by soil and climate for growing grapes. Oysters are affected by water temperature (the lower the temperature, the firmer the meat), salinity (higher salinity creates a cleaner, sharper flavor), and the vegetation on which they feed. And they can have a different taste and texture in different seasons.

"Nationally, Cape oysters are distinguished by how clean-tasting they are," says Walton, who also works at the Woods Hole Oceanographic Institution Sea Grant. Wellfleet, on the Outer Cape, is the flagship of New England's oyster industry. But in the last decade, several other parts of the Cape — Brewster, Barnstable, Chatham, and Dennis — as well as Duxbury and Martha's Vineyard have also become known for oysters.

Cultivating oysters means daily visits to the flats, where they grow in mesh bags strung along poles. In mild, dry weather, life on the flats can be very peaceful. But when the wind whips up and the temperature drops, it's time for action. Though some oysters can survive a winter at the bottom of the sea, protected by sand, many growers take their oysters out of the water to protect them from ice that forms on the surface. They store them in pits, or temperature- and humidity-controlled chambers, between 32 and 40 degrees Fahrenheit. During this period, oysters stop growing and build up glycogen, a carbohydrate that sustains them through the cold weather and gives them their sweet taste.

Some in the business say this is one reason for the claim that oysters are best eaten in months containing an 'r.' Another is the fact that oysters reproduce in the warmer months, which changes their physiology and, in turn, their flavor. Deep-water oysters spawn at 72 degrees, but in the shallow flats of Wellfleet, the water is warmer, so the oysters spawn early. An exception is Duxbury oysters, which never spawn.

Though the prime season starts around September, there's never a bad time to eat oysters. So enjoy the full variety of what our local waters offer. And wash them down with a glass of crisp, clean white wine.

Every October, we celebrate the Outer Cape's shellfishing traditions at Wellfleet OysterFest, featuring oyster chowder, oyster stew, and other local bivalve specialties. A two-day oyster shucking competition is a highlight. Visit www.wellfleet oysterfest.org.

Traditional Oyster Stew

S E R V E S 4

24 oysters
6 tablespoons unsalted butter
1/2 cup leeks or onions,
  cut into 1/8-inch dice
1/4 cup celery, cut into 1/8-inch dice
3 cups whole milk
1 to 2 teaspoons kosher salt, or to taste
1/2 teaspoon pepper, to taste
Toasted common crackers (see Page 65)
1 teaspoon coarsely chopped parsley
1 teaspoon chopped fresh chives

1. Shuck the oysters, removing all shell fragments and reserving the juices. In a bowl, combine the oysters and the juices; refrigerate.
2. In a large saucepan, melt the butter and cook the leeks or onions and celery for about 8 minutes or until the vegetables soften.
3. Add the oysters and their juices with the milk. Sprinkle with salt and pepper. Turn the heat to low and let the milk warm and the oysters cook for 8 to 10 minutes. Do not let the milk boil.
4. Use a slotted spoon to divide the oysters among 4 warm soup plates. Ladle the broth into the bowls. Float 4 to 6 common cracker halves in the stew and sprinkle with parsley and chives. Serve at once.
Note: To prepare the common crackers, split them horizontally.

Brush with soft butter, place on a baking sheet, and toast in a 350 degree oven for about 5 minutes or until golden brown.
☙ ANDREA PYENSON
adapted from Jasper White

Lobster Stew

S E R V E S 4

Linda Greenlaw, a former swordfish boat captain, was at the helm of the Hannah Boden, a sister ship to the doomed Andrea Gale, when the ship survived what came to be called "the perfect storm." "Recipes From a Very Small Island," which she wrote with her mother, Martha, is deeply rooted in the daily cooking of Isle au Haut, Maine, which is home to generations of Greenlaws. "Around here, cooking's more than a hobby," says Linda. "There aren't any restaurants, so if you want to eat you're just gonna have to cook." Linda uses female lobsters for this stew so she has roe to add to the broth.

4 lobsters, female if possible
  (1 1/2 pounds each)
1/2 cup (1 stick) unsalted butter
6 cups whole milk
2 cups heavy cream
1/3 cup Madeira or medium-dry sherry
1 tablespoon chopped fresh tarragon
Salt and white pepper, to taste

1. In a large pot, steam or boil the lobsters for 12 minutes. Drain, and when cool enough to handle, pick the meat, reserving the green tomalley and any red roe that you get from the bodies and tails. Discard the black intestinal strip from the tails.

Cut the meat into bite-size pieces.
2. In a soup pot, melt the butter. Add the tomalley and roe and cook for 2 minutes over medium heat, crushing the roe with the back of a spoon to break it into small bits. Add the lobster meat and cook for 3 minutes.
3. Add the milk, cream, and wine. Bring to a boil, stirring often. Add the tarragon, salt, and pepper. When the mixture comes to a boil, the stew is ready to ladle into bowls.
☙ JONATHAN LEVITT
adapted from Martha and Linda Greenlaw's "Recipes From a Very Small Island" (Hyperion)

Mussels in Spicy Tomato Sauce

S E R V E S 6

You can capture shellfish juices by steaming them in the pot, as we do with mussels in white wine. Then the cooking liquid and the sweet mussel meat go into spicy tomato sauce. It's an economical way to cook, both in terms of cost and time, since preparing either mussels or clams for a crowd is relatively inexpensive, and the cooking is carefree.

1 cup white wine
3 thyme sprigs
4 peppercorns
Bunch of parsley stems
1 small onion, halved
4 pounds mussels

1. In a large flameproof casserole, bring the wine to a boil. Tie the thyme, peppercorns, parsley, and onion in cheesecloth and drop the

bundle into the pot. Add the mussels, cover the pan, and steam them over high heat for 3 to 5 minutes or until they open.

2. Use a slotted spoon to lift out the mussels and transfer them to a bowl. Discard any unopened mussels. Line a strainer with several layers of cheesecloth. Strain the broth through the cheesecloth. Set aside 1 1/2 cups of the broth.

SAUCE

1 tablespoon olive oil
1 onion, finely chopped
Salt and freshly ground black
* pepper, to taste*
2 cloves garlic, chopped
1/2 teaspoon crushed red pepper
1 can (15 ounces) imported
* whole tomatoes, crushed*
4 ripe plum tomatoes, cored and chopped
4 thick slices crusty bread, toasted
3 tablespoons chopped fresh parsley
3 tablespoons chopped fresh basil

1. In a large flameproof casserole, heat the oil and cook the onion with salt and pepper over medium heat, stirring often, for 10 minutes or until it is soft.

2. Add the garlic, crushed red pepper, canned tomatoes, and fresh tomatoes. Cook them over medium heat, stirring often, for 5 minutes. Add the reserved mussel cooking liquid and bring the sauce to a boil. Turn down the heat and simmer the sauce for 10 minutes. Taste for seasoning and add more salt and pepper if necessary. Add the reserved mussels and reheat them for 1 minute.

3. Place a piece of toasted bread in each of 4 shallow bowls. Spoon the mussels and sauce on top. Sprinkle with parsley and basil and serve at once.

Y SHERYL JULIAN AND JULIE RIVEN
adapted from "The Way We Cook" (Houghton Mifflin)

Greek Fish Soup
SERVES 6

In 1996, Chrissi Pappas opened the Ipswich Shellfish Fish Market in Ipswich, Massachusetts, where she sells seafood and lots of prepared and specialty foods. A favorite is her fish soup. She uses thick pieces of boneless haddock (she doesn't want them to fall apart during cooking) with rice, carrots, onion, potato, and celery. Pappas cooks the soup quickly so the vegetables retain their natural color because, she says, "you first eat with the eyes; then you taste."

2 quarts water
1 large carrot, coarsely chopped
1 large stalk celery, coarsely chopped
1 medium onion, coarsely chopped
1 medium russet potato, coarsely chopped
3/4 cup raw converted white rice
3/4 cup olive oil
2 1/2 pounds haddock, cut into thirds
Salt and pepper, to taste
Several sprigs fresh parsley,
* coarsely chopped*

1. In a large stock pot, bring the water to a boil. Add the carrot, celery, onion, potato, rice, and oil. Return to a boil and then cook on medium-high heat for 10 minutes, stirring often.

2. Add the haddock and cook on medium-high heat for 10 minutes; turn the heat to low and continue cooking for 10 minutes. Stir very gently.

3. Remove the pot from the heat and add salt and pepper. Ladle into large bowls and garnish with parsley.

Y EMILY SCHWAB
adapted from Chrissi Pappas

"You first eat with the eyes; then you taste," says Chrissi Pappas of Ipswich Shellfish Fish Market in Massachusetts. She makes her Greek fish soup with pieces of boneless haddock, cut thick so it doesn't fall apart.

A charter boat crew member gets a laugh out of skate caught on a Cape Cod fishing trip. Most American skate is caught and processed in New England.

Skate
Your Way to Richer Chowder

BY KEN RIVARD, Globe Correspondent

Not long ago, inspired by Jasper White's "50 Chowders," I made my way to the fresh seafood case at my favorite supermarket. The New England Fish Chowder recipe I had in mind called for 3 pounds of fresh cod or haddock.

Then I saw the skate: gleaming fans of rose-colored flesh, completely boned and on sale for little more than half the price of cod.

Although skate is plentiful in the Pacific, most American skate is caught and processed in New England. Ninety-five percent of the catch is shipped to France, where seafood lovers know a good thing when they taste it.

When cooked, the fish offers a firm-textured white flesh that comes apart in long, slender blades, with a flavor made sweet from a diet of clams, mussels, and other mollusks.

Like sharks and rays, skate are cartilaginous fish. Only the wings (actually, dorsal fins) are eaten. Lacking kidneys, skate process wastes through their skin, producing urea, which can rapidly decompose into ammonia if the fish isn't handled properly.

Always ask to sniff a sample fillet before buying, and reject it if it smells of anything other than clean, cold seafood. Diehard fans maintain that a faint scent of ammonia is acceptable and can be eliminated by soaking the fish in a solution of water and lemon juice, but why bother? If it doesn't smell perfect, don't buy it.

Treat skate the same way you would raw shrimp: Keep it quite cold and use it when you get home or, at very most, a day later.

The reward for incorporating skate into chowder is a delicious, rich soup with a beguiling flavor and satisfying texture. Unlike cod, which is prone to flaking apart if stirred during reheating, skate tends to hold its shape.

The most reliable way of acquiring skate is to call your favorite fish purveyors (even at a chain supermarket) and tell them you're interested in buying some for a dinner in several days so they can order it for you. They'll check with their seafood suppliers each day to see if it's available. You might get lucky and get it on the day of your dinner; 24 hours in advance is also fine, as long as you keep it cold. Be sure to request that it be boned and skinned (if a market carries skate, this is almost automatic, but it doesn't hurt to check).

If skate fails to appear, you can always go the traditional route and use cod.

SKATE CHOWDER

Skate Chowder
SERVES 8

4 ounces meaty salt pork, rind removed
   and cut into 1/3-inch dice
2 tablespoons unsalted butter
2 medium onions (about 14 ounces),
   chopped into 3/4-inch dice
1 tablespoon chopped fresh thyme
2 dried bay leaves
2 pounds new potatoes, scrubbed,
   sliced 1/2-inch thick
5 cups fish stock (or 4 cups high-quality,
   low-sodium chicken stock plus 1 cup
   clam juice)
Coarse salt and freshly ground pepper
3 pounds boned skate wings, trimmed
   of any silver skin and cut into chunks
   4 to 5 inches wide
1 1/2-2 cups light cream at room
   temperature (use heavy cream for the
   original, super luxurious version)
2 tablespoons chopped fresh
   flat-leaf parsley
2 tablespoons minced fresh chives

1. Heat a 4- to 6-quart heavy pot over low heat, and add the diced salt pork. Once it has rendered a few tablespoons of fat, increase the heat to medium, and cook until the pork is a crisp, golden brown. Using a slotted spoon, transfer the cracklings to a small ovenproof dish, leaving the fat in the pot. Set the cracklings aside to use as a garnish. If the fat in the pot is smoking, turn off the heat and let the pot cool for a few minutes before proceeding to the next step, otherwise the onions will singe as soon as they're added.

2. Add the butter, onions, thyme, and bay leaves to the pot and sauté over medium heat, stirring occasionally with a wooden spoon, until the onions are soft, but not brown, about 8 minutes.

3. Add the potatoes and stock. If the stock doesn't cover the potatoes, add just enough water to cover them. Turn up the heat and bring to a boil, cover, and cook the potatoes vigorously until they're soft on the outside, but still firm in the center, about 10 minutes. If the stock hasn't thickened slightly, smash a few of the potatoes against the side of the pot to release their starch, and cook a few minutes longer. Reduce the heat to low and season assertively with salt and pepper. You almost want to over season the dish so you don't have to stir in more salt and pepper after you've added the cream.

4. Lower the pieces of skate into the liquid. Cover and cook over low heat for 5 minutes, then remove the chowder from the heat and allow to sit for 10 minutes (the skate will finish cooking during this time).

5. Gently stir in the cream and taste for salt and pepper. Try to disturb the fish as little as possible. If you are not serving the chowder within the hour, let it cool for a bit uncovered, then refrigerate; cover the chowder after it has chilled completely. Otherwise, let it sit for up to an hour at room temperature, allowing the flavors to meld. Don't skip this last step; it's essential to give the flavors time to mingle.

6. When ready to serve, reheat the chowder over low heat; don't let it boil. Warm the cracklings in a low-temperature oven (200 degrees) for a few minutes.

7. Use a slotted spoon to mound chunks of skate, onions, and potatoes in the center of large soup plates or shallow bowls. Ladle the creamy broth around them. Scatter the warm cracklings over the individual servings, sprinkle with parsley and chives, and serve.

☙ KEN RIVARD
adapted from Jasper White's "50 Chowders" (Scribner)

ASK THE COOKS

Flour Power

Q Is there a way to make hearty, creamy clam and fish chowders without using any flour as a thickening agent?

ANSWER Old recipes did not call for thickeners. They required a special technique: Cook everything to death. If you simmer a pot of fish and potatoes for as long as most grandmothers did, the fish breaks down into tiny pieces, combines with the starch from potatoes, and eventually the pot thickens nicely.

In Colonial New England, when fishermen made chowders aboard their boats, the pots contained little besides fish and water. They were thickened with rocklike biscuits called hardtack, which were crushed and stirred into the pot. We suggest instead using starchy russet potatoes and adding heavy cream.

☙ SHERYL JULIAN AND JULIE RIVEN

FROM THE FRENCH WORD "CHAUDIÈRE" — denoting the caldron used in the 18th century to make these homey stews — chowders have lots of flavor and broth, so that the liquid in the bottom of the bowl can be enjoyed with crushed crackers. Oyster crackers are universally preferred for this end-of-bowl ritual, but our choice is the Bent's Common Cracker — a large, dry, airy cracker (www.bentscookiefactory.com) made in Milton, Massachusetts, for two centuries. To serve these everyday crackers, carefully halve them, brush them with soft butter, and toast the buttered sides lightly in a gentle oven until the edges brown. The recipe comes from Fannie Farmer, who ran a cooking school in 19th-century Boston and knew a thing or two about chowders and what went with them. ☞ SHERYL JULIAN AND JULIE RIVEN

Clam Chowder with Turkey Kielbasa
SERVES 4

Modern chowders generally are stewy affairs, but they're light stews, not out of place at a beach-house supper.

2 tablespoons olive oil
1 shallot, finely chopped
4 leeks, white part only, finely chopped
1 stalk celery, finely chopped
About 6 ounces turkey kielbasa, thinly sliced
2 cups clam broth
3 cups water
1 pint chopped clams
1 cup heavy cream
1 teaspoon dried thyme
Salt and pepper, to taste

1. In a large flameproof casserole, heat the oil and cook the shallot, leeks, and celery over low heat, stirring often, for 15 minutes or until the vegetables are soft but not brown. Add the kielbasa and cook for 5 minutes more.
2. Pour in the broth, water, and clams. Bring to a boil, lower the heat, and simmer for 15 minutes. Add the cream and thyme and return to a boil. Turn the heat to low and cook for 2 minutes. Add salt and pepper. Ladle the chowder into bowls and serve at once.
❧ SHERYL JULIAN AND JULIE RIVEN

Red Clam Chowder
SERVES 4

We live in chowder country, which means that we can take all the liberties we want with the standard bowl of fish or clams in a creamy broth. That freedom includes serving clam chowders that old-timers in some parts of New England don't consider chowders at all. Manhattan and Rhode Island clam chowders contain tomatoes instead of cream and are traditionally made from ground quahogs. Many seafood markets sell these ground clams.

Note: For a spicy sausage version of this chowder, cut 8 ounces chorizo or linguica sausage into 1-inch pieces and add to the pot with the tomatoes.

2 tablespoons olive oil
1 Spanish onion, finely chopped
1 carrot, finely chopped
1 stalk celery, finely chopped
4 plum tomatoes, peeled, seeded, and chopped
1 clove garlic, finely chopped
1/4 teaspoon crushed red pepper
2 cups water
2 cups clam broth
1 pint ground or chopped clams
2 Yukon Gold potatoes, peeled and cut into 1/4-inch cubes
2 tablespoons chopped fresh thyme
Salt and black pepper, to taste

1. In a large flameproof casserole, heat the oil. Add the onion, carrot, and celery. Cook over medium heat,

stirring often, for 5 minutes.

2. Add the tomatoes, garlic, crushed pepper, water, clam broth, and clams. Bring to a boil, turn the heat to medium-low, cover the pot, and simmer the mixture for 45 minutes. Add the potatoes and return the chowder to a boil. Lower the heat, cover the pot, and simmer for 20 minutes, or until potatoes are tender.

3. Sprinkle with thyme, salt, and black pepper. Ladle the chowder into bowls and serve at once.

▼ SHERYL JULIAN AND JULIE RIVEN

Mussel Chowder
SERVES 4

4 pounds mussels, rinsed well
1 cup white wine
1 tablespoon canola oil
2 tablespoons butter
1 Spanish onion, coarsely chopped
2 carrots, finely chopped
1/2 fresh fennel bulb,
    cored and finely chopped
1 stalk celery, finely chopped
1 shallot, finely chopped
3 sprigs of fresh thyme
1 clove garlic, finely chopped
1/8 teaspoon saffron threads
1 cup water
1/2 cup heavy cream
Salt and pepper, to taste

1. Remove the beards from the mussels. Discard any shells that are cracked.

2. In a pasta pot, combine the mussels and wine. Cover with the lid and steam over high heat, shaking the pan several times, for 5 minutes or until the mussel shells open. Discard

any mussels that do not open.

3. Remove the mussel pot from the heat. With a slotted spoon, lift out the mussels and transfer them to a bowl to cool. Line a large strainer with several layers of cheesecloth. Pour the mussel cooking liquid through the cloth; set aside.

4. In a large flameproof casserole, heat the oil. When it is hot, add the butter. When the butter melts, add the onion, carrots, fennel, celery, shallot, and thyme sprigs. Cook over medium heat for 10 minutes, stirring often, or until the vegetables soften. Add the garlic and saffron. Cook for half a minute. Pour in the mussel cooking liquid and water. Bring to a boil. Cover the pan and simmer for 5 minutes. Remove the thyme sprigs.

5. When the mussels are cool enough to handle, remove them from the shells. Add the mussels to the pot along with the cream, salt, and pepper. Heat just until the mixture is bubbling at the edges. Ladle the chowder into bowls and serve at once with crusty bread.

▼ SHERYL JULIAN AND JULIE RIVEN

Noank Clam Chowder
SERVES 4-8

The range of chowders available in New England varies from the clear southern New England broth to a tomato-laced Rhode Island variety and the better known cream-based version found in Boston. From the Seahorse Tavern in Noank, Connecticut, comes this traditional

clam chowder made without milk or cream.

3 ounces salt pork, finely diced
1 stalk celery, chopped
1 large leek (white and pale green parts),
    chopped
1 medium onion, chopped
6 cups bottled clam broth
4 cups water
4 medium potatoes, diced
3 cups chopped hard-shell clams
2 tablespoons chopped fresh thyme
2 tablespoons chopped fresh parsley
Salt and pepper, to taste

1. In a large soup pot over medium heat, render the salt pork for 15 minutes or until the pork is crisp. Remove the pork from the pan and drain on paper towels.

2. Add the celery, leek, and onion. Cook, stirring often, for 8 minutes or until the vegetables are softened.

3. Add the clam broth, water, potatoes, clams, and thyme. Bring to a boil, lower the heat to medium-low, and cover the pan. Simmer gently for 15 minutes or until the potatoes are tender.

4. Remove from heat and let chowder rest, partially covered, at room temperature for at least 1 hour, or refrigerate for up to 2 days.

5. To serve: Bring to a boil gently. Add more broth or water if the chowder seems too thick. Stir in the parsley and add salt and pepper to taste. Sprinkle the salt pork on top and serve with oyster crackers.

▼ CLEA SIMON
adapted from Brooke Dojny's "The New England Clam Shack Cookbook" (Storey Publishing)

Newer New England Fish Chowder

SERVES 4

When Jasper White first hauled out old New England fish chowder recipes and offered them up in perfect renditions in his former Boston restaurant, Jasper's, food lovers went crazy. White seemed to give adventurous cooks permission to experiment with this food and then fall in love with it again. His chowder involved meaty salt pork, fish, homemade fish stock, and oodles of heavy cream.

So where would the chowder go if experimentation were taken a step further? Perhaps standing it on end would mean redefining the dish first. Does there have to be lots of liquid and not much fish? We could reinvent the dish, we thought, by simply inverting the proportions. We would set poached fish and potatoes in the thinnest pool of creamy, brothy essence and flavor it with pancetta (a meaty Italian bacon). Yes, we know, it's nothing like old-fashioned "chowdah," but even our best-loved New England dishes need a little dusting off now and then.

5 peppercorns
5 coriander seeds
2 cloves garlic
1 bay leaf
2 slices pancetta, finely chopped
2 tablespoons butter
1 Spanish onion, finely chopped
2 cups whole milk
2 cups bottled clam broth
6 Yellow Finn or Yukon Gold potatoes, thinly sliced
Salt, to taste
1 1/2 pounds skinless, boneless halibut, cod, or pollock, cut into 4 pieces
1 cup heavy cream
4 long sprigs of parsley (for garnish)

1. In a piece of cheesecloth, place the peppercorns, coriander seeds, garlic, and bay leaf. Tie it into a bundle and set it aside.

2. In a flameproof casserole over medium heat, cook the pancetta, stirring often, until it is golden brown. Using a slotted spoon, transfer the pancetta to a plate, and pour off any excess fat. Add the butter to the pan and cook the onion over medium-high heat, stirring often, for 10 minutes.

3. Add the milk, clam broth, potatoes, cheesecloth bag, and salt. Bring to a boil, lower the heat, and simmer the potatoes for 10 minutes or until they are tender but not falling apart. Using a slotted spoon, transfer the potatoes to a plate. Continue cooking the broth for 10 more minutes.

4. Add the fish to the broth and poach it over medium heat for 5 minutes or until it is firm and opaque.

5. Remove the sack of spices. Add the cream to the pan and bring it to a boil.

6. To serve: In each of 4 shallow soup bowls, set some potato slices at the bottom, arrange a piece of fish on top and add more potato. Garnish with pancetta. Add the remaining pancetta to the creamy broth and taste it for seasoning. Add more salt and pepper if you like. Ladle the sauce in a pool around the fish and garnish each dish with a parsley sprig. Serve at once.

➤ SHERYL JULIAN AND JULIE RIVEN

Vietnamese Hot and Sour Scallop Soup

SERVES 6

Nina Simonds, the Salem, Massachusetts-based cookbook author and Asia correspondent for Gourmet magazine, makes this soup for her family and serves it with just a bowl of rice. She loves the lemongrass and lime juice, the contrast of the briny scallops with the sweet and spicy broth, and the freshness of the cilantro and the bean sprouts. The soup is easy to make.

3 stalks lemongrass, trimmed, and the outer stalks removed
1 teaspoon olive oil
2 1/2 tablespoons chopped shallots
2 medium tomatoes, cored, seeded, and cut into 1/4-inch dice
1 can (17 ounces) straw mushrooms, blanched briefly in boiling water and drained
1 tablespoon sugar
5 cups water
1 pound sea scallops, rinsed and drained
5 1/2 tablespoons fish sauce, or to taste
3 1/2 tablespoons lime juice
1 teaspoon dried chili flakes, or to taste
1 1/2 cups bean sprouts, rinsed and drained
3 tablespoons chopped fresh cilantro

1. Split the lemongrass in half lengthwise, cut into 3-inch lengths, and smash with the flat side of a knife or cleaver.

2 . Heat a heavy pot or casserole over medium-high heat for 20 seconds or until hot. Add the oil and heat about 20 seconds. Add the shallots and lemongrass and stir for 15 seconds or until fragrant.

3. Add the tomatoes, mushrooms, and sugar. Stir-fry for about 1 minute. Add the water and bring to a boil. Reduce the heat to medium-low and simmer uncovered for 10 minutes.

4. Meanwhile, holding the knife on the diagonal, cut the scallops through the thickness into three slices.

5. Add the scallops, fish sauce, lime juice, and chili flakes to the soup. Simmer for about 2 minutes, until the scallops turn opaque. Using tongs, lift out the lemongrass and discard it. Stir the bean sprouts and cilantro into the soup. Cook 1 minute or just until they are heated through. Ladle into bowls.

▼ JONATHAN LEVITT
adapted from Nina Simonds's "Spices of Life: Simple and Delicious Recipes for Great Health" (Knopf)

Shrimp Broth with Snow Peas and an Egg
SERVES 4

The pot that simmers on our back burner most nights contains chicken and vegetables or just vegetables in a well-flavored chicken-based broth.

If supper is going to consist solely of soup, we figure, the pot should contain plenty of protein. With the same reasoning, you can simmer a heavenly stock from shrimp shells, left after peeling the firm shellfish. Instead of discarding the shells, simmer them with aromatic vegetables, tomatoes, and a little hot chili paste and the mixture will clear your sinuses.

1 pound large unshelled shrimp
1 teaspoon vegetable oil
1 onion, quartered
1 carrot, quartered
2 plum tomatoes, quartered
1 stalk celery (with leaves),
*   cut into fourths*
5 stalks fresh parsley
1/2 teaspoon hot red chili paste
1 bay leaf
8 cups water
1 teaspoon distilled white vinegar
4 eggs
1/4 pound snow peas,
*   halved on a diagonal*
Salt, to taste

1. Peel the shrimp, reserving the shells.

2. In a large saucepan, heat the oil. Cook the onion, carrot, tomatoes, celery, and parsley over medium heat, stirring often, for 5 minutes.

3. Stir in the chili paste, bay leaf, shrimp shells, and water. Bring to a boil, lower the heat, and simmer for 20 minutes.

4. Meanwhile, bring a deep skillet of water to a boil. Add the vinegar. Break each egg into a small custard or tea cup. When the water is at a rolling boil, holding a cup right

above the water, tip out the egg. Continue until all 4 eggs are in the water. Lower the heat at once and let the eggs simmer for 3 to 4 minutes or until the whites are firm. Spoon boiling water over the eggs if the eggs are not covered with water. Don't worry about ragged edges on the eggs.

5. With a slotted spoon, lift the eggs from the water and transfer to a plate. With scissors, trim the ragged edges of the eggs. Turn a bowl upside down over the plate to keep the eggs warm.

6. Strain the broth into a clean saucepan. Add the snow peas and shrimp and cook for 2 minutes or until the shrimp turn pink. Taste for seasoning and add salt, if you like.

7. Ladle the soup into 4 large bowls. Add a poached egg to each one and serve at once.

Note: To serve the soup with eggs whisked in egg-drop-soup style, omit the poached eggs. Instead, beat 2 eggs lightly. When the shrimp are cooked, turn off the heat. Add the eggs in a thin stream in circles around the edges of the pan. With a fork, stir the soup gently. Spoon it into bowls and serve.

▼ SHERYL JULIAN AND JULIE RIVEN

Portuguese Boil

SERVES 6

One-pot dishes are as old as cooking itself and still the easiest way to make dinner, especially in summer. In New England, the sea provides the main ingredient. This clambake at home is made with only three ingredients: clams, potatoes, and sausage. The dish has been prepared on Cape Cod since Portuguese fishermen settled there a century ago. To make a leaner version, use turkey-based linguica or chorizo instead of the pork sausages.

6 pounds clams for steaming
3/4 cup water
2 pounds linguica or chorizo sausage
6 medium Yukon Gold or Yellow Finn potatoes

1. Soak the clams in several changes of cold water, scrubbing them with a brush if they're gritty. Drain the clams.

2. In a large soup kettle, combine the clams and water. Slice the sausage into 2-inch pieces and add them to the kettle.

3. Cut the potatoes into 1/2-inch pieces and place them on top of the clams and sausages. Cover the pot and set it over high heat. As soon as you see steam coming from the top of the pot, turn the heat to medium-low and cook for 15 minutes or until the potatoes are tender.

4. Discard any unopened clams. Serve the dish in deep bowls, ladling broth over the clams, sausages, and potatoes. Put out crusty bread.

▼ SHERYL JULIAN AND JULIE RIVEN

GREEK FISH SOUP

VIETNAMESE SOUP WITH SCALLOPS

GADGETS

Dutch Ovens

Dutch ovens are perfect for soups and stews. Our favorite is made of enamel-coated cast iron, a combination good for the heat-retaining qualities of the iron and the easy cleanup of the porcelain, which also won't react with acids the way uncoated iron can. Classic enameled cookware is heavy and pricey, though, leading some companies to market lighter-weight and sometimes cheaper entrants. Here are some pots that we recommend:

Le Creuset French Oven (www.lecreuset.com/usa): Classic design, beautiful colors, solid construction, great heat retention. Quite heavy.

Staub La Cocotte (www.staubusa.com): Can withstand higher oven temperature than Le Creuset and has dimples on underside of lid to facilitate basting. Lid doesn't fit as tightly as other pots.

Lodge Enamel Dutch Oven (www.lodgemfg.com): Also has dimples under lid, and can handle higher oven temperature than Le Creuset. Limited color availability; side handles get hot quickly.

All-Clad Provence (www.allclad.com): This cast aluminum pot is lightweight, nonstick, easy to clean, and able to withstand metal utensils and higher heat. Doesn't retain heat as well as cast iron; tighter fit in the oven.

Innova Color Cast (www.innova-inc.com): Less than half the price of other enameled cast iron lines, with similar performance. Plain design; 25-year warranty is shorter than the lifetime guarantees of other pots.

Emile Henry Flame Stewpot (www.emilehenry.com): The stoneware is lighter weight than iron, has dimples under lid, can go in the microwave, and can be used with metal utensils. Cannot be used on induction stovetops; slightly harder to clean than other pots.

☞ JOE YONAN

LE CREUSET FRENCH OVEN   EMILE HENRY FLAME STEWPOT   INNOVA COLOR CAST

ALL-CLAD PROVENCE

Shack Bouillabaisse SERVES 4

1 small baguette for croutes
1/4 cup olive oil
3 cloves garlic, finely chopped
1 medium leek (about 3 ounces) white
*   and light green part, cut in half length-*
*   wise and then across in 1/2-inch slices*
1 small bulb fennel (6 ounces), quartered,
*   cored, and thinly sliced (discard top but*
*   save a few fronds for garnish)*
1 stalk celery (1 1/2 ounces),
*   cut thinly on a diagonal*
1 medium onion (6 ounces) thinly sliced
1 bay leaf
1/2 teaspoon fennel seeds, crushed
1 teaspoon saffron threads
1 cup dry, acidic white wine
2 cups fish stock or lobster broth
1 small can (14.5 ounces) Italian plum
*   tomatoes, cut in long, thin slices (julienne)*
*   with their juice*
Freshly ground black pepper
1/4 teaspoon cayenne pepper
1 tablespoon very finely sliced orange rind,
*   white pith removed*
2 live 1 to 1 1/4 pound hard-shell lobsters
12 littleneck clams
8 large shrimp
16-20 mussels
12 medium (20-30 size) sea scallops

1. Make the croutes: Set the oven to 350 degrees. Slice the baguette on a bias into 1/3-inch-thick pieces. Line the slices on a cookie sheet and bake for 10 to 15 minutes until golden brown and dry.
2. In a large (4-6 quart) heavy soup pot, heat 2 tablespoons olive oil over medium heat. Add the garlic, leek, fennel, celery, onion, bay leaf, fennel seeds, and saffron. Cover and cook for about 12 minutes, stirring occasionally, until the vegetables are soft but not brown.
3. Add the wine, fish stock, and tomatoes with their juice and bring to a boil. Season with black pepper and add the cayenne and orange rind. Reduce the heat and simmer for 15 minutes. Transfer this vegetable and broth mixture to a medium (2-3 quart) sauce pot and keep warm while you prepare the seafood. (Or refrigerate for up to a day.)
4. Cut the lobster into 6 pieces (split body, claws, and tail). Scrub the clams, peel and de-vein the shrimp (do not remove tail fins), de-beard and scrub the mussels, and pick over the scallops, removing the strap and shell fragments. If you made the broth ahead, warm it.
5. Place the large heavy pot over medium high heat. Add the remaining 2 tablespoons olive oil and when it smokes, add the lobster claws and body (not the tails) along with the clams and cook for about 2 minutes, until the shells turn red. Add the broth mixture and bring to a boil, then lower to a simmer. Cover and cook for 3 minutes. Add the lobster tails and cook, covered, for 1 more minute. Add the shrimp and mussels. Cover and cook 1 more minute. Add the scallops. Cover and cook 1 more minute and remove from the heat.
6. Let the mixture sit for 2 minutes; season with salt and pepper, if needed. Divide the shellfish evenly into 4 soup plates, ladle in the broth and vegetables, and garnish with the fennel fronds. Serve with croutes.

❥ JASPER WHITE

JASPER WHITE
A James Beard award winner trained by the Culinary Institute of America, this New England sea-food guru gained fame in the 1980s for the innova-tive fine dining served at his first Boston restaurant, Jasper's. Later, he took a simpler approach with Summer Shack, a chain of clam shack-inspired eateries. His cookbooks include "Lobster at Home" and "50 Chowders" (Scribner).

"At Summer Shack our all-shellfish bouillabaisse is not quite authentic, but who cares? It's delicious."

baked shrimp

monkfish piccata

grilled bluefish with mustard

seared swordfish

halibut with prosciutto

grilled lobster

sea clam pie

En

We

don't just hunt in New England. We fish. We dig for clams, mussels, and oysters. Some of us even have lobstering permits. And if we don't catch our ocean-inspired meals ourselves, we do the next best thing: We go straight to the dock or the local fish monger, where the fish looks as though it just swam in from the sea, because it probably did. Often, when we sit down to our boiled lobster dinner, our simple but celebratory clambake, our skillet-fried cod or our seared swordfish, we feel a connection to the waters that surround us. And we remember why we have chosen to live here. Despite the winters.

trees

OVEN-FRIED FISH AND CHIPS

Taking in Takeout Fish

🐟 BY SHERYL JULIAN, Globe Staff, and JULIE RIVEN, Globe Correspondent

In England, fish and chips come wrapped in newspaper, and the first thing you do is douse them with malt vinegar. Yes, they're greasy, but they're irresistible, particularly in an out-of-the-way chip shop where the employees don't understand your accent any better than you understand theirs.

The English taught us to appreciate fish this way, and to this day, fish and chips are all over New England menus. But if you fry the dish at home, someone will ask you days later if you were making fish — no matter how fancy your kitchen ventilation system.

Fried fish and chips aren't good for you, anyway. So leave the Fryolator to the restaurant cooks, and coat your fillets with crumbs and slip them into a very hot oven. The idea is not to abandon the dish, just make the leap from old England to modern times.

Oven-Fried Fish and Chips
SERVES 6

We've been making this fish and chips for years, never as successfully as with panko, Japanese white bread crumbs. The potatoes, which are cut into spears and roasted with olive oil and salt, can go with all kinds of dishes.

Olive oil (for sprinkling)
2 russet potatoes, unpeeled and cut
    into 1/2-inch spears
Salt and pepper, to taste
1 clove garlic, halved
4 scallions, cut into thirds
1/4 cup fresh parsley leaves
1/2 cup panko
Pinch of paprika (optional)
1 1/2 pounds cod fillets,
    cut into 3-inch pieces
Olive oil (for drizzling)

1. Set the oven at 450 degrees. Have on hand 2 rimmed baking sheets. Oil 1 sheet (for the fish).
2. In a bowl, toss the potatoes with enough oil to barely coat them. Arrange the potatoes on the dry baking sheet, cut sides up. Sprinkle them with salt.
3. Transfer the potatoes to the hot oven and bake them for 30 to 40 minutes or until they are golden brown. Halfway through cooking, use a wide metal spatula to turn the spears.
4. In the bowl of a food processor fitted with the steel blade, pulse the garlic, scallions, parsley, salt, and pepper until finely chopped. Add the panko and pulse twice. Transfer the crumbs to a large, flat bowl. Stir in a pinch of paprika if you like.
5. Sprinkle the crumbs over the fish, drizzle the fish with oil, and set the pieces on the oiled baking sheet. Transfer the fish to the hot oven. Bake the fish for 15 minutes or until it is golden brown and firm to the touch. Slide the fish under the broiler for 1 minute to make the top golden. Serve at once with the chips.

🐟 SHERYL JULIAN AND JULIE RIVEN
adapted from "The Way We Cook" (Houghton Mifflin)

Supplies of cod off New England shores began to dwindle in the late 1980s, but some say they are coming back. All agree you should know where your fish comes from. Dayboat, hook-caught cod is a good choice.

Cod in a Skillet

SERVES 4

You'd be surprised what a grand meal you can make in a single skillet. We often advise home cooks who are shopping for new equipment to buy as large and heavy a skillet as they can afford; it's so essential to nightly meals that it should go on must-have lists above a tea kettle. In a good skillet with a heatproof handle, you can brown food on top of the stove and then transfer it to the oven. Or do it all on top.

2 tablespoons olive oil
3/4 pound green beans, trimmed
  and halved
1 1/2 pounds cod, cut into 4 serving pieces
Salt and pepper, to taste
4 ears corn, kernels cut from the cob
1/2 cup bottled clam broth
1 tablespoon butter, cut into 4 pieces
3 tablespoons chopped fresh parsley

1. In a large skillet, heat the oil. Add the green beans and cook over medium-high heat for 2 minutes, stirring often. Push the beans to the sides of the pan and tuck the cod in the center. Sprinkle with salt and pepper. Brown the cod over medium heat for 5 minutes on one side.
2. Using a spatula, turn the cod. Add the corn and broth. Bring to a boil, cover the pan, and cook over medium-low heat for 2 minutes or until the fish is cooked through and the vegetables are tender.
3. Place a pat of butter on each piece of fish. When it melts, sprinkle the fish with parsley. Serve at once.
☙ SHERYL JULIAN AND JULIE RIVEN

Cornmeal Scrod

SERVES 4

When coated with cornmeal, scrod (small cod or haddock) becomes crusty in the oven. Serve the fish with roasted potatoes and creamy coleslaw.

1 1/2 tablespoons vegetable oil
1/2 cup yellow cornmeal
1/3 cup dry breadcrumbs
Salt and pepper, to taste
1 egg
2 tablespoons water
4 pieces (6 ounces each) scrod fillet

1. Set the oven at 450 degrees. Brush a rimmed baking sheet with oil.
2. On a plate, combine the cornmeal, breadcrumbs, salt, and pepper. In a shallow bowl, mix the egg and water.
3. Dip the fish in the egg mixture and cornmeal mixture to coat both sides. Transfer the fish to the baking sheet.
4. Bake cod for 10 minutes, turning halfway through cooking, or until it is golden brown and cooked through.
☙ LISA ZWIRN

Gray Sole Roasted in Parchment with Spring Vegetables

SERVES 6

Roasting fish inside parchment paper is an old method that produces flavorful fish with very little fat. The fish steams inside the paper, which puffs as it cooks. We use gray sole, but any of the flatfish, including flounder, would work well. You can't get very much fish inside the paper, so plan to serve 2 packets per person. Though fresh artichokes are glorious in this dish, we recommend frozen, which are easy to cook, as are frozen edamame, which are edible soy beans.

Butter (for the parchment)
1 1/2 pounds small red potatoes
2 cups frozen shelled edamame
2 packages (10 ounces each)
  frozen artichoke hearts
1 bunch scallions, trimmed and cut into
  long, thin pieces
12 skinless fillets of gray sole or other
  thin white fish fillets (about 2 pounds)
Olive oil (for drizzling)
3 tablespoons chopped fresh thyme
Salt and pepper, to taste
2 lemons, cut into thin slices

1. Set the oven at 450 degrees. Have a roll of parchment paper on hand. Cut a 15-inch piece of parchment and fold it lengthwise. Cut the paper into a heart shape by using the folded side as the middle of a half-heart. Cut as large a curve as you can to make a half-heart and open the heart on the counter. Rub the inside with butter. Make 11 more hearts.
2. In a saucepan with a steamer insert and several inches of cold water, steam the potatoes, covered, for 10 to 15 minutes or until tender. Remove the potatoes from the pan. When they are cool enough to handle, slice them thinly; set aside.
3. Add the edamame to the steamer. Add more water if some of it has

evaporated. Cover the pan and steam over high heat for 5 minutes. Remove the edamame from the steamer insert; set aside. Add more water to the saucepan and bring to a boil. Drop in the artichokes. Let them bubble for 3 to 4 minutes or until they are cooked through. Drain and rinse with cold water.

4. To prepare the packets, place the parchment buttered side up on a work surface. Layer the ingredients on one side of the fold, keeping them to within 1 inch of the edge. Divide the potatoes, artichokes, edamame, and scallions among the papers. Add fish to each one. Drizzle with oil, thyme, salt, and pepper. Place a few lemon slices on top.

5. To seal the packets, fold the empty part of the heart over the fish. Starting at one end of the edge, fold the edges over onto themselves. The fold will be about 1 1/2 inches and look like tight pleating. Continue with the other packets. Set them on 2 rimmed baking sheets.

6. Cook in the hot oven for 15 minutes or until the paper begins to turn golden brown at the edges and you can hear the insides of the packet sizzling.

7. Serve the packets at once, instructing guests to use their forks to pierce the top of the paper to open it.

❧ SHERYL JULIAN AND JULIE RIVEN

Stuffed Flounder

SERVES 4

Butter (for the dish)
1 tablespoon butter
1 small onion, quartered
1 clove garlic, halved
25 round buttery crackers (such as Ritz)
1/2 cup fresh parsley leaves
Salt and pepper, to taste
3 zucchini, thinly sliced on the diagonal
8 skinless flounder fillets
(about 1 1/2 pounds)
Olive oil (for sprinkling)

1. Set the oven at 400 degrees. Have on hand a 10-inch baking dish. Lightly butter the dish.

2. In a small skillet, melt the 1 tablespoon butter and cook the onion and garlic over medium heat, stirring often, for 10 minutes.

3. In a food processor, work the crackers to make crumbs. Transfer to a bowl. Without rinsing the processor, work the onion and garlic with the parsley until finely chopped. Return the crumbs to the processor with salt and pepper. Work the mixture just until it comes together.

4. Arrange half the zucchini, overlapping the slices, in the baking dish.

5. Set the fish on the counter, skinned side up (the skinned sides are the darker sides). Divide the cracker mixture among the fish, shape the mixture into a log near the wide end of each fillet. Roll up, beginning at the wide end. Set the fish in the baking dish, seams down. Tuck any filling that falls out back into the rolls at the sides.

6. Sprinkle the fish with salt and pepper. Cover the fish with the remaining zucchini, making overlapping rows. Sprinkle with oil, salt, and pepper.

7. Bake the fish for 25 minutes or until it is cooked through and the zucchini are golden at the edges. Serve at once, spooning the zucchini and the juices in the pan on each plate beside the fish rolls.

❧ SHERYL JULIAN AND JULIE RIVEN

Buying fish isn't much different from buying lettuce. You pick through the pile of lettuce until you find a head with bright green leaves. Obviously, you can't pick through a tray of haddock fillets, but you can ask the fishmonger to check his case for thick cuts that satisfy you.

Seared Haddock with Parsnips, Bacon, and Brussels Sprouts

SERVES 4

Some New Englanders seem to have forgotten what makes haddock distinctive. So often it's sloshed in batter and used interchangeably with cod and pollock for fish and chips that its flavor is deep-fried out of existence.

Yet many chefs, fishermen, and diners prize firm haddock fillets, including those at Duckworth's Bistro in Gloucester, Massachusetts, where chef-owner Ken Duckworth lets local tastes influence his recipes.

"A lot of people in Gloucester, when they eat fish, they sauté cabbage with it," he says. Duckworth's seared haddock over Brussels sprouts, bacon, and caramelized parsnips is richly nuanced and less predictable than haddock and cabbage, yet it's a tip of the hat to an older tradition.

1 medium parsnip
12 Brussels sprouts
4 ounces slab bacon, cut into cubes
  (or thick sliced bacon)
3/4 cup chicken stock
4 tablespoons butter, softened
Salt and pepper, to taste
12 ounces skinless, boneless haddock,
  cut into 2 pieces
2 tablespoons canola oil
1 tablespoon chopped parsley
Juice of 1/2 lemon

1. Set a cast-iron skillet over low heat to begin warming.
2. Halve the parsnip lengthwise and slice thinly on the diagonal.
3. Bring a saucepan of water to a boil. Halve the Brussels sprouts, leaving root ends intact. Drop them into boiling water, and cook for 5 minutes or until tender. Transfer to ice water and set aside.
4. In another skillet, render the bacon. Remove it from the pan. Add the parsnips and cook for 8 minutes or until the slices are tender and browned. Add the Brussels sprouts, reserved bacon, and stock. Bring to boil.
5. Remove parsnip mixture from the heat. Add 2 tablespoons of the butter, salt, and pepper. Keep warm.
6. Sprinkle the fish with salt and pepper. In the cast-iron skillet that has been warming, heat the oil and cook the fish flesh side down for 3 minutes. Turn and cook 2 more minutes. Fish should barely flake.
7. Divide the fish and vegetables between 4 plates; keep warm.
8. In a small saucepan, heat the remaining 2 tablespoons butter until the foam subsides. Add salt, pepper, parsley, and lemon juice. Pour it over the fish and serve.

❦ RACHEL ELLNER
adapted from Duckworth's Bistro

Skate Wings with Brown Butter

SERVES 4

Skate is the wing of a ray fish, and in the market it looks like a big fan. Some people think the taste of skate is similar to scallops, and certainly it has the mild, slightly gelatinous, sweet taste of a large sea scallop. In France the fish is called raie, and the classic cooking method is to sauté the fish and serve it with browned butter. We found that skate does well under the broiler, where it turns golden quickly without being flipped over. Heat a little butter with capers until they brown, and pour the dark liquid over the skate with lots of lemon juice. Skate takes so little time to cook that you should have the plates ready when you slip it under the broiler.

Olive oil (for the pan)
1 3/4 pounds skinless, boneless skate wings
1 tablespoon olive oil
Salt and pepper, to taste
2 tablespoons butter
2 tablespoons small capers
Juice of 1/2 lemon
1 tablespoon chopped fresh parsley

1. Turn on the broiler. Set a rack 6 inches from the element. Have on hand a large roasting pan or a jelly-roll pan that will not buckle under the heat of the broiler. Add a few drops of oil to the pan. Use your fingers to rub the oil all over the pan.
2. Set the skate in the pan and use the 1 tablespoon of oil to rub the top of the fish. Sprinkle it with salt and pepper. Slide the fish under the broiler. Cook the fish for 5 to 8 minutes without turning it until it is browned and cooked through (cut into the middle to check this).
3. Meanwhile, in a small saucepan, melt the butter. Add the capers and cook the butter until it browns. Set

the pan aside.

4. Divide the fish among 4 dinner plates, add a spoonful of the brown butter to each piece of fish. Sprinkle with lemon juice and parsley. Serve at once with steamed potatoes.

☛ SHERYL JULIAN AND JULIE RIVEN

Halibut Wrapped in Prosciutto
Ⓢ Ⓔ Ⓡ Ⓥ Ⓔ Ⓢ ④

At Caffe Umbra in Boston's South End, chef Laura Brennan wraps a thick, square piece of halibut with Italian prosciutto. She begins by cooking the fish in a hot skillet, then finishes it in the oven. The apple and-leek garnish enriched with heavy cream is a kind of stove-top gratin.

2 tablespoons butter
4 small leeks, white part only, halved and thinly sliced
Salt and pepper, to taste
4 Granny Smith apples, peeled, cored, and thinly sliced
1/4 cup heavy cream
1 3/4 pounds boneless halibut, cut at least 1-inch thick
8 slices prosciutto
1 tablespoon olive oil

1. In a skillet, melt the butter. Add the leeks, salt, and pepper and cook over medium-low heat for 10 minutes, stirring often, or until the leeks are tender. Stir in the apples, cover the pan, and continue cooking, stirring occasionally, for 20 minutes or until the apples are tender.

2. Pour the cream into the pan at the edges. Stir well and set the pan aside, off the heat.

3. Set the oven at 350 degrees.

4. Cut the halibut into 4 even-sized pieces. Sprinkle them with salt and pepper. Wrap 2 pieces of prosciutto around each piece of fish, securing it at the sides with toothpicks, or tie the fish with string.

5. Have on hand a cast-iron or other heavy-based skillet with a heatproof handle. Add the oil. When the oil is hot, add the fish in 1 layer. Sear it for about 2 minutes on a side. Turn the fish only when it releases easily from the bottom of the pan.

6. Transfer the skillet to the oven and cook the fish for 10 minutes more or until it springs back when pressed gently with a fingertip.

7. Meanwhile, stir the apple mixture over medium-high heat until it is hot and the cream is absorbed by the fruit.

8. Divide the apple mixture among 4 dinner plates. Top with the fish. Remove the toothpicks or string and serve at once.

☛ SHERYL JULIAN AND JULIE RIVEN
adapted from Laura Brennan

Monkfish Piccata
Ⓢ Ⓔ Ⓡ Ⓥ Ⓔ Ⓢ ④

It's been made fun of, called bad names, and dumped overboard. Now monkfish is no longer overshadowed by cod or haddock and is enjoying well-deserved recognition. It's no longer "poor man's lobster," especially not for fishermen like Paul Cohan, who runs Sasquatch Smokehouse in

Gloucester, Massachusetts.

2 pounds monkfish
1 cup flour
1 cup grated Parmesan or Romano cheese
1 teaspoon dried oregano
1 clove garlic, finely chopped
Salt and pepper to taste
2 eggs, lightly beaten
1/3 cup olive oil, or more if necessary
Juice of 1 lime

1. Remove the membrane on the fish. Cut fish into 3/4-inch-thick rounds.

2. In a bowl, combine the flour, cheese, oregano, garlic, salt, and pepper. Toss well to mix.

3. Put the egg into a shallow bowl. Dip the pieces of fish in the egg, then in the flour mixture. Dredge them well all over.

4. In a large deep skillet, heat the oil, adding enough to make a thin film in the bottom of the pan. When it is hot, add the fish and cook over medium heat for 3 minutes on a side or until golden brown.

5. Arrange on a platter and sprinkle with lime. Serve at once.

☛ RACHEL ELLNER
adapted from Paul Cohan

STRIPED BASS WITH ORANGE ALE SAUCE

That Bass Deserves a Beer

BY ANN CORTISSOZ and JOE YONAN, Globe Staff

Chef Daniel Bruce is a wine guy. He drew on 13 years as chef of the Boston Wine Festival when he opened Meritage in the Boston Harbor Hotel and organized its menu not by course but around six categories of wine. So why is Bruce, in his elegant dining room with its spectacular harbor view, up to his toque in bottles of beer, choosing brews to go with some specially created dishes?

Because even Bruce acknowledges that matching food with ales and porters is easier, perhaps even more natural, than with pinots and cabs. "You're much more limited in your wine selections than with beer," he says. "Beer is much more versatile to begin with. It's more powerful. The flavors are right there on the tongue."

Bruce thinks beer and food matching should happen with the food first. Perhaps the easiest way to think about a match is through balance — the weight of the beer, the effect on your palate, can either match the weight of the dish or can offset it. Bruce can make his dishes beer-friendly by using beer in the sauces, like the orange-ale sauce accompanying the bass on the next page.

APPETIZERS • SALADS • SOUPS & STEWS • **ENTREES** • PASTA & RICE • SANDWICHES

Striped Bass with Orange Ale Sauce

SERVES 4

Pair this dish with Hitachino white ale or Foret organic French ale. Ginger in the refreshing Hitachino and Foret's pepper and maltiness complement the sauce.

8 tablespoons butter
1 leek, thinly sliced
2 ears fresh corn, kernels removed
Salt and pepper, to taste
1 cup orange juice
1/2 cup pale ale, such as Samuel Adams
1 tablespoon olive oil
4 pieces skinless, boneless striped bass
  (3 1/2 ounces each)

1. In a medium saucepan, heat 4 tablespoons of butter over medium heat. Add the leek and cook for 5 to 6 minutes or until tender. Add corn, salt, and pepper and cook for 2 minutes. Keep warm.
2. In a small saucepan over medium-high heat, combine orange juice and ale. Bring to a boil, lower heat to medium, and simmer steadily until the liquid reduces to about 1/2 cup. Turn the heat to low.
3. Cut the remaining 4 tablespoons of butter into cubes. Whisk them into sauce until incorporated. Remove from heat and cover to keep warm.
4. In a large skillet with a heat-proof handle, heat the oil over high heat. Sprinkle the fish with salt and pepper. Fry for 8 to 10 minutes, turning once, or until golden brown. Remove from heat and let cool.

5. Divide the leek mixture among 4 plates, top each with a bass fillet, and pour orange sauce over.
⌐ ANN CORTISSOZ AND JOE YONAN
adapted from Daniel Bruce

Grilled Mackerel

SERVES 4

Chased north by the bluefish and striped bass, large shoals of mackerel arrive off the coast of Massachusetts by the middle of May and then keep swimming north to Maine and Nova Scotia, where they spend the summer. Atlantic mackerel is a member of the Scombridae family, a group that includes bluefin tuna, bonito, and albacore. Like sharks, these fish must swim continuously to stay afloat and ventilate their gills. This constant motion makes the flesh dark and oily, and it spoils if not kept ice cold.

With their sleek, tapered bodies, velvety smooth iridescent skin, and wavy black stripes, mackerel are among the most beautiful fish in the sea. They are also, along with salmon, trout, and tuna, particularly high in heart-healthy omega-3 fatty acids. Because of its oil, mackerel is not only grilled but also smoked.

1/2 teaspoon grated lemon rind
1 1/2 tablespoons lemon juice
Salt and pepper, to taste
1/3 cup olive oil
2 tablespoons chopped fresh thyme
4 whole fresh mackerel (1 pound each)
2 tablespoons vegetable oil
3 lemons, thinly sliced (to make 20 slices)

1. In a bowl, whisk the lemon rind and juice, salt, and pepper. Add the olive oil a little at a time, whisking constantly. Stir in the thyme. Set vinaigrette aside.
2. With a sharp paring knife, make shallow slits at 2-inch intervals along the fish on both sides. Brush them all over with vegetable oil and sprinkle with salt and pepper. Sprinkle the cavities with salt and pepper, as well, then place two lemon slices in each one. Close cavities, then place 2 lemon rounds on the sides of each fish. Use kitchen string to tie the fish at 2-inch intervals, securing the lemon slices.
3. Light a charcoal grill or set a gas grill to medium high. When the coals turn gray, lightly oil the grill rack. Grill the fish, covered with the lid, for 6 minutes on a side, or until the fish is cooked through.
4. Transfer the fish to a large platter, snip off and discard the strings, and serve fish with the lemon vinaigrette.
⌐ JONATHAN LEVITT
adapted from Alan Wulf of Wulf's fish market in Brookline, Massachusetts

Grilled Bluefish with Mustard Glaze

SERVES 4

Juice of 1/2 lemon
2 teaspoons Dijon mustard
1 clove garlic, finely chopped
Salt and pepper, to taste
2 tablespoons olive oil
2 pounds boneless bluefish (skin intact),
  cut into 4 even-sized pieces
Olive oil (for brushing)
1 lemon, cut into wedges (for serving)

MACKEREL

1. In a bowl, whisk the lemon juice, mustard, garlic, salt, pepper, and oil.

2. Place the fish on a deep platter and pour the lemon marinade over it. Turn the fish to coat it all over. Refrigerate for 20 minutes.

3. Prepare a charcoal or gas grill. Brush the rack with oil. When the grill is hot, set the fish on the rack, skin side down. Cover with the lid and cook the fish for 8 to 10 minutes or until it flakes easily when you test the thickest part with the tip of a knife. It is not necessary to turn the fish.

4. Transfer to a platter, garnish with lemon, and serve at once.

▼ SHERYL JULIAN AND JULIE RIVEN

GADGETS Indoor Smokers

Even in the dead of winter, a couple of nifty devices can transform your kitchen into a wood-smoking paradise. Both of these products work especially well with fish, whose delicate flesh seems to invite the smoke to come on in and stay awhile.

First up: the **Camerons Stovetop Smoker** (www.cameronssmoker. com) that looks and acts like a roasting pan with a fitted lid. A couple tablespoons of finely ground wood chips go in the bottom, a drip tray and rack go on top of the chips, and the food sits on the rack. As

long as you don't overcook it, your dinner stays beautifully moist.

If you don't think you'll smoke foods often enough to justify buying another gadget, check out the **Savu food smoker bag** (www.savu.fi/english/). This little piece of Finnish ingenuity takes all the guesswork out of smoking. You put the food in a pan, put the pan in the heavy-duty foil bag, seal it, and bake. The bags don't generate quite as much smoke or flavor as the stovetop smoker, but their ease of use and price make them worth checking out.

☞ JOE YONAN

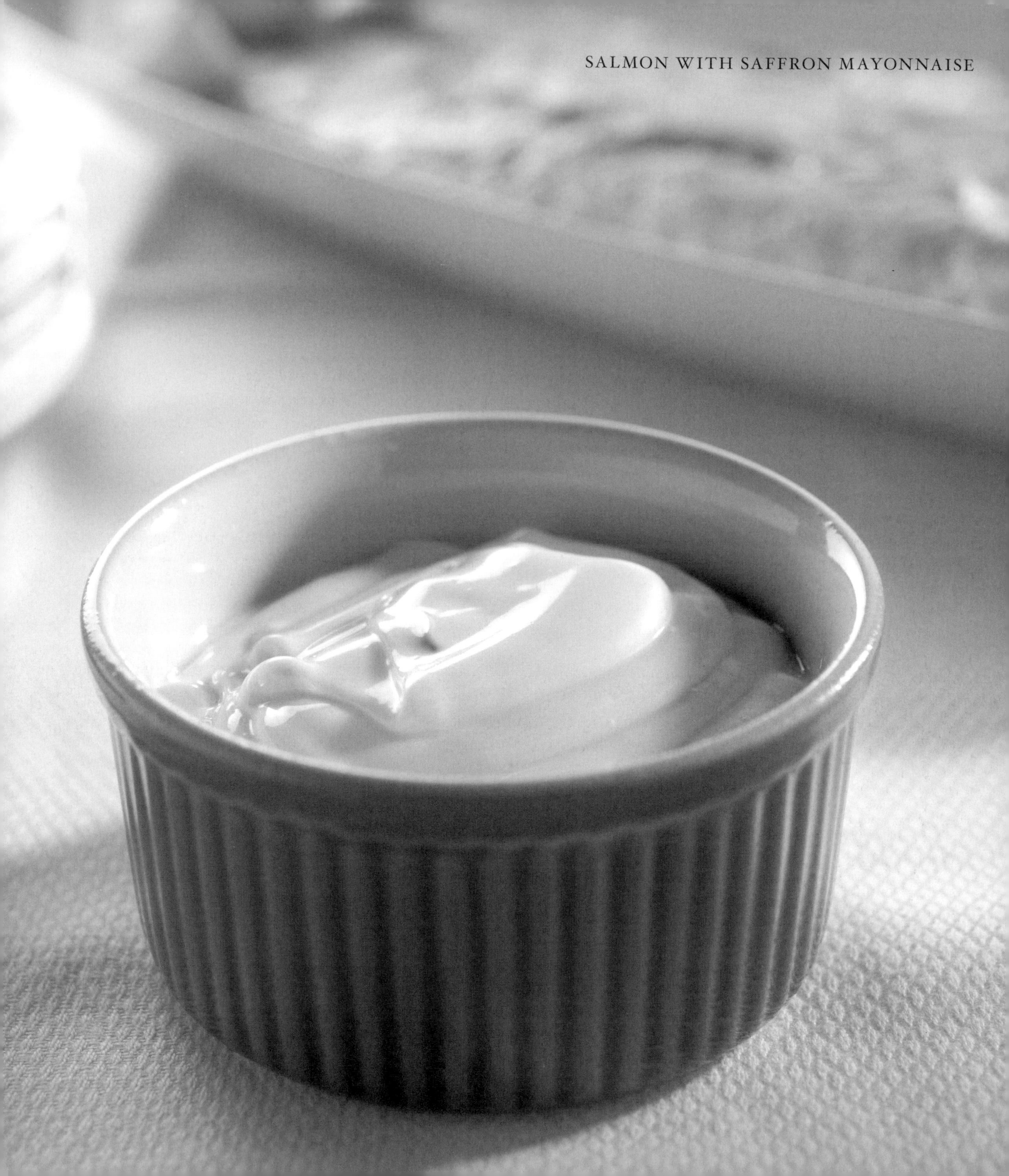

SALMON WITH SAFFRON MAYONNAISE

Oven-Poached Salmon with Saffron Mayonnaise

SERVES 6

Although poaching fish on the stovetop requires an aromatic liquid, if you seal the fish tightly — here it's wrapped in foil and parchment — the juices in the salmon provide enough liquid to produce moist fish.

1 whole salmon fillet (2 1/2 to 3 pounds)
Olive oil (for sprinkling)
Salt and pepper, to taste
1/8 teaspoon saffron
2 tablespoons boiling water
1 cup mayonnaise
1 tablespoon lemon juice, or to taste
1 lemon, cut into 6 wedges (for garnish)

1. Set the oven at 450 degrees. Have on hand a large platter slightly longer than the salmon. Using foil, shiny side down, line a rimmed baking sheet that is large enough to hold the salmon flat. Rub the foil with oil. Set the salmon on the foil, skinned side up. Sprinkle with oil, salt, and pepper. Cover the salmon with a sheet of parchment paper.
2. Cover the paper with foil, shiny side down. Crimp the top and bottom pieces of foil together to make a tight seal. Set the baking sheet in the oven and poach the salmon for 15 to 20 minutes or until it is cooked through.
3. Meanwhile, in a small bowl, mix the saffron and boiling water. Set it aside for 5 minutes.
4. In a bowl, stir the mayonnaise until it is smooth. Add the saffron mixture and lemon juice. Taste the mayonnaise and add more salt, pepper, or lemon juice if you like. Cover with plastic wrap and refrigerate.
5. When the salmon is ready, carefully open the layers of foil and paper. Let the salmon cool slightly. Use the foil as a sling to slide the salmon onto the platter.
6. Garnish the fish platter with the lemon wedges. Serve with the saffron mayonnaise.

▼ SHERYL JULIAN AND JULIE RIVEN

Seared Swordfish with Tomato-Olive Salsa

SERVES 4

Seafood aficionados know that swordfish is at its sweetest in the waning weeks before the species swims south to warmer waters. The great sword has spent several months in the north, and by fall, the flesh has a meaty quality. As such, the rich fish responds well to the hot fire of a charcoal grill, but if the backyard is already tidied up for the season, a thick swordfish steak will also hold up under the broiler or in a searing skillet.

What the dense sword loves and needs beside it is a strong garnish: sauces made with olives and capers, sweet-and-sour fruit combinations, fleshy roasted bell peppers and garlic, or fennel and orange. These bold accompaniments can be salsa-like, as in a tomato-olive sauce served with seared swordfish, or saucy, like an intense garlicky bell pepper mixture that complements broiled fish.

1 pint cherry tomatoes, quartered
1 tablespoon capers
1/4 cup chopped Kalamata or other
  black olives, pitted and chopped
4 scallions, finely chopped
2 tablespoons chopped fresh oregano
6 tablespoons olive oil
2 tablespoons red wine vinegar
Salt and pepper, to taste
1 3/4 pounds thick swordfish,
  cut into 4 pieces

1. Set the oven at 425 degrees. Have on hand a cast-iron or other heavy skillet with a heatproof handle.
2. For the salsa: In a bowl, combine the tomatoes, capers, olives, scallions, and oregano. Sprinkle the salad mixture with 4 tablespoons of the oil, then the vinegar, salt, and pepper. Toss gently and set aside.
3. Heat the skillet over high heat. Add the remaining 2 tablespoons of oil. Sprinkle the fish with salt and pepper. When the pan is hot but not smoking, carefully add the fish. Sear on one side for 1 to 2 minutes or until golden. Turn the fish and sear the other side for 1 to 2 minutes.
4. Transfer the skillet to the hot oven. Cook the fish for 5 minutes or until it is cooked through but still moist.
5. Arrange the fish on 4 dinner plates. Spoon the salsa on top and beside the fish and serve at once.

▼ SHERYL JULIAN AND JULIE RIVEN

Swordfish with Braised Fennel in Orange Juice

SERVES 4

3 tablespoons olive oil
1 3/4 pounds thick swordfish,
    cut into 4 pieces
Salt and pepper, to taste
1 Spanish onion, thinly sliced
1 fennel bulb, trimmed and thinly sliced
Grated rind and juice of 1 orange
1 tablespoon chopped fresh thyme

1. Turn on the broiler. Use 1/2 tablespoon of the oil to grease a broiler pan. Set the fish in the pan and use 1/2 tablespoon of the oil to rub the top of the fish. Sprinkle with salt and pepper.

2. In a large skillet, heat the remaining 2 tablespoons of oil. Add the onion and fennel with salt and pepper. Cook, stirring often, for 5 minutes.

3. Pour the orange juice and rind into the fennel mixture. Cover with a lid and continue cooking the mixture, stirring occasionally, for 10 minutes or until the onion and fennel are almost melted. Turn off the heat.

4. Broil the swordfish pieces without turning for 8 minutes or until the fish is cooked through but still moist.

5. Arrange the fish on 4 dinner plates. Spoon the braised fennel on the fish, sprinkle with thyme, and serve at once.

❦ SHERYL JULIAN AND JULIE RIVEN

SWORDFISH WITH TOMATO-OLIVE SALSA

FIRST-TIME FISH-BUYER'S GUIDE

Try to buy whole fish, so you can ascertain general appearance. Fillets are difficult to assess, and preservatives can keep them looking fresh. Whole fish can be filleted by a friendly fishmonger.

1. Make sure the eyes are clear.

2. Make sure the gills are red or, with nonfarmed fish such as striped bass, pale.

3. Ask whether the fish is sushi-grade.

4. If you don't like the looks of the fish, walk away in an operatic display of disgust. ☙ TED WEESNER JR.

Tuna Au Poivre with Green Beans

SERVES 4

Crack peppercorns by placing them between several layers of paper towels and forming them into a bundle. With a cast-iron skillet, pound the peppercorns until they are coarsely cracked. Use kosher or sea salt for this dish.

Kosher or sea salt, to taste
1 pound haricots verts
  or other slender green beans
1 3/4-pound piece tuna,
  cut at least 1 inch thick
2 tablespoons cracked peppercorns
2 tablespoons olive oil
1/4 red onion, thinly sliced
Leaves from 3 stalks flat-leaf parsley
1 tablespoon red wine vinegar
Ground pepper, to taste

1. Bring a large saucepan of water to a boil. Add a pinch of salt and drop in the beans. Let the water return to a boil. Cook the beans for 2 minutes or until they are cooked through but still bright green.
2. Tip the beans into a colander and rinse them with cold water until they are cold. Set them aside.
3. Set the oven at 450 degrees. Have on hand a cast-iron or other heavy-based skillet with a heatproof handle.
4. Cut the tuna into 4 even-sized pieces. Rub them with salt and cracked peppercorns, pressing them into the flesh.
5. Heat the skillet until it is quite hot. Add 1 tablespoon of the oil. Add the tuna pieces in 1 layer. Sear them for about 2 minutes on a side. Turn the tuna only when it releases easily from the bottom of the pan.
6. Transfer the skillet to the oven and cook the fish for 4 to 5 minutes more or until it is cooked through but still pink in the center.
7. In a bowl, combine the haricots verts or green beans, onion, and parsley leaves. Sprinkle with the remaining 1 tablespoon of oil, vinegar, salt, and ground pepper. Toss gently but thoroughly.
8. Set a piece of tuna on each of 4 dinner plates. Add green bean mixture and serve at once.

❧ SHERYL JULIAN AND JULIE RIVEN

Tuna Kebabs

SERVES 4

Taking a cue from street vendors in Asia and the Middle East who sell grilled skewered meat, otherwise known as kebabs, you can turn out a quick and easy dish that takes well to a variety of seasonings, marinades, and glazes, none of which you have to make yourself. Because the pieces of fish are bite size (maximum two bites), they cook quickly.

2 tablespoons soy sauce
1 tablespoon rice vinegar
1 teaspoon toasted sesame oil
1 teaspoon powdered wasabi mixed with
  1 teaspoon water
1 pound tuna steak, about 1 inch thick,
  cut into 1-inch chunks
4 10- or 12-inch bamboo skewers,
  soaked in water for 10 minutes

1. Prepare the grill or broiler for medium-high heat.
2. In a shallow dish, combine the soy sauce, vinegar, sesame oil, and wasabi. Add the tuna, toss to coat, and let stand at room temperature for about 10 minutes.
3. Thread tuna onto skewers and place kebabs on a lightly oiled rack. Grill or broil, turning the skewers a few times, until the tuna is browned and either partially or fully cooked through (as desired), from 5 to 10 minutes.

❧ LISA ZWIRN

Did you know?

The discriminating diner should angle for nothing less than a "day-boat" fish. Denoting fresh and local seafood, the term means that the item was caught by an angler who went out in the morning and came back in the evening with his or her catch, rather than by large fishing boats that troll for days or more and hold seafood in refrigerated tanks until landfall.

☛ ALISON ARNETT

Cooking Lobster

There are two ways to boil lobsters — the deep-water method and the shallow-water method. Shallow works so well that it hardly seems worthwhile to wait for a large pot of water to boil for the deep method.

Fill the bottom of a large kettle with several inches of water and bring it to a boil. Quickly add the lobsters and put the lid on. Cook 1 1/2-pound lobsters for 8 minutes; cook 2-pound lobsters for 10 minutes. At the end of cooking, the shells should be very firm and bright red.

Lift out the lobsters with tongs and pile them onto a board. (Put paper towels around the edges to catch the juices.) Let the lobsters cool.

With a large sharp knife, make a slash in the underside of the tail and hold the lobster over a bowl so the juices drain. Crack the claws with a mallet or with the dull side of a cleaver.

Remove the meat and use as directed.

☛SHERYL JULIAN

LOBSTER WITH POTATO SALAD

Basic Lobster Dinner

BY SHERYL JULIAN, Globe Staff, and JULIE RIVEN, Globe Correspondent

Supper at the beach is delightfully predictable. It's always some variation on the clambake: chowder, lobster, and clams, luscious sides of potato salad and slaw. Even poorly equipped kitchens in rental houses have a big pot for this event.

So many generations of New Englanders have dined on this menu that many fish markets will boil the lobsters and clams to order. The sides, of course, are all available by the pound at the supermarket.

When it's time to take a break from the sun and surf, you can dash into the kitchen and whip up tomorrow's beach feast, one dish here, and one dish there. Then set out the plastic cutlery and head to the table.

Boiled Lobsters with Butter

SERVES 6

6 live lobsters (1 1/2 to 2 pounds each)
2 sticks butter, melted

1. Bring 2 large pots of water to a boil. Add the lobsters and return the water to a boil. Adjust the heat so the water boils gently and cook the lobsters for 15 to 20 minutes (about 10 minutes per pound) or until they are bright red and cooked through.
2. Remove the lobsters from the pots and transfer them to the sink. Crack the claws with nut crackers and use kitchen shears to cut through the shell on the underside of each lobster. Drain any excess water into the sink and then set the lobsters on a platter. Serve with butter for dipping.

— SHERYL JULIAN AND JULIE RIVEN

Potato Salad with Red Onion

SERVES 6

16 small red potatoes
2 tablespoons cider vinegar
Salt and pepper, to taste
4 stalks celery, halved lengthwise
  and thinly sliced
1/2 small red onion, finely chopped
1 bunch scallions, finely chopped
1/4 cup chopped fresh parsley
3/4 cup mayonnaise
2 tablespoons warm water,
  or more if needed
1 teaspoon sugar

1. In a saucepan fitted with a steamer insert, steam the potatoes, covered, over several inches of boiling water on medium-high heat for 15 to 20 minutes or until the potatoes are tender. Transfer them to a large shallow bowl.
2. When the potatoes are still quite hot, slice them into 1/4-inch-thick rounds. Sprinkle them with vinegar, salt, and pepper. Cool.
3. Add the celery, onion, scallions, and parsley.
4. In a small bowl, whisk together the mayonnaise, 1 tablespoon of the water, sugar, salt, and pepper. The dressing should pour easily. Add the remaining water, 1 teaspoon at a time, if necessary.
5. Pour the dressing over the potatoes and toss gently. Taste for seasoning and add more vinegar, salt, and pepper if you like.
6. Serve at once or cover with plastic wrap and refrigerate. If the salad seems too thick, add 1 to 2 teaspoons of vinegar and stir gently.

— SHERYL JULIAN AND JULIE RIVEN

Lobster on the Grill

BY CATHERINE WALTHERS, Globe Correspondent

If you think of boiled lobsters as an old dog in need of a new trick, you might try grilling them. In about the time it takes to boil or steam one, a lobster can be grilled on the backyard barbecue for an entirely different — and memorable — experience.

Cooking lobster in a pot is straightforward and basic. That's part of its appeal. Grilling lobster maintains the simplicity, but combines a smoky fire with the sweet meat. The lobster is infused with a hint of smoke and other flavors you brush onto the meat during grilling. The result is a large platter of charred red lobster halves, which can be garnished with lemon wedges and herbs to make an impressive presentation.

New Englanders are so hooked on boiled lobsters that convincing them of the fine techniques for grilling lobster vary. While most cooks split the lobster down the middle before grilling, some grill it whole. Some prefer the claws attached; others remove the claws and cook them separately. Some split the lobsters live and throw them on the grill; others blanch them first.

Chef Allen Bohnert, formerly of the Red Rock Bistro in Swampscott, Massachusetts, splits the live lobster lengthwise and separates the claws for blanching, then seasons the lobster body and tail with salt and pepper. He places the halves on the grill flesh side up.

Bohnert finds that the claws and knuckles dry out on the grill, so he cooks them completely in a pot, while the tails grill for 8 to 10 minutes. In the other camp are the cooks who keep the claws on. Restaurateur Jasper White, author of "Lobster at Home," suggests covering the claws with a metal pie plate or small roasting pan so they cook evenly with the tail.

Either way, split the lobster as close to grilling time as possible. And be sure not to turn it shell side up during cooking. Hard-shelled lobsters fare better on the grill; during molting season, soft-shelled lobster need attention and a little less cooking time.

When choosing a crustacean, "Look for a lively disposition," advises Jasper White. "Liveliness equals strength equals freshness." Another indicator of freshness is long antennae. Short feelers often mean the lobster has been swimming in the tank with its cannibalistic colleagues for more than a few days. — ELAINE MCARDLE

Grilled Lobsters
SERVES 2

2 lobsters, 1 1/2 to 2 pounds, with hard shells if available
2 tablespoons butter, melted, or oil
Salt and pepper, to taste
2 lemons, cut into wedges (for serving)

1. Light a charcoal grill.
2. Split the lobsters live down the middle on the underside with a large sharp knife, starting at the head between the eyes, and continuing down the tail. Use poultry shears or scissors to help cut through the tail and body. Keep the knuckles and claws attached. Remove and discard the head and intestinal vein, green tomalley (liver), and roe from each lobster.
3. Place the lobsters, shell side down, on a rimmed baking sheet. Brush each side of the lobster half, including the claws, with butter or oil. Sprinkle the exposed tail meat with salt and pepper.
4. When the fire is ready, place the halves on the grill, shell side down. Place metal pie shells or shallow roasting pans over the claws and knuckles. Cover the grill and cook for 8 to 10 minutes without turning the lobster over. Baste the exposed tail meat at least twice during grilling. The lobster is done when the meat is opaque or creamy white.
5. Place the lobsters on a large platter and garnish with lemon. Serve them with nut crackers for opening claws and legs, or crack them before serving.
— CATHERINE WALTHERS

Clambake on the Grill

SERVES 12

New England really doesn't have the smoking and barbecuing lore of other parts of the country, but what is native is the clambake. Boston chef Jim Fahey is enthusiastic about adapting the shore tradition — where shellfish might be buried in seaweed and cooked in a pit over a wood fire — to the backyard. His bake is "more of a memory than an actual recipe."

Fahey likes to find a gunnysack — an old rice sack with no dyes on it is a good choice, he says. In it, he'll layer parboiled potatoes and corn on the cob, then clams, then mussels. Sliced Portuguese sausage, or linguica, goes over that; the salt from the sausage will season all the ingredients.

3 pounds small red or Yukon gold potatoes
12 to 16 ears of corn,
shucked and cut in half
1 medium-sized gunnysack without dye
1 large roasting pan
(sturdy disposable is fine)
3 pounds Portuguese sausage (linguica),
sliced thickly
3 dozen littleneck clams, scrubbed
3 dozen mussels, scrubbed
6 to 8 live lobsters, about 1 pound each
1 pound (2 sticks) butter, melted

1. In a large, kettle-style grill, build a fire with hardwood charcoal on the bottom and chunks of wood on the top. Light the fire and allow it to burn down.

2. Wash but don't peel the potatoes, then place them in a large pot of water. Bring to boil and cook for 8 minutes. Drain.

3. Refill the pot with water, bring to boil, and add the corn. Cook for 8 minutes, then drain.

4. When the fire has burned down, push the glowing coals to one side, and place a large roasting pan on the other side, away from the coals.

5. Open the gunnysack and place it in the roasting pan on the grill. In the gunnysack, layer the potatoes, corn, sliced sausage, clams, and mussels, in that order. Close the grill cover and allow the contents of the sack to cook. Check after about 20 minutes, to see if the mussels and clams have opened up.

6. In the meantime, bring another large pot (or two, if the pot is not large enough to hold all of the lobsters) of water to a boil, and plunge in the live lobsters. (Freeze them for 30 minutes first to dull their senses, if you like.) Cook until they are bright red, then drain, split in half, and clean the interiors.

7. When the mussels and clams have opened, empty the contents of the gunnysack into a large pan or bowl, reserving the juices. Put the split lobsters on top of the mussel mixture, and pour melted butter and the reserved juices over all. Serve with crusty bread and coleslaw on the side.

ALISON ARNETT
adapted from Jim Fahey

New England Stovetop Clambake

SERVES 4

Called lobster bake in some regions, clambake in others, and still made in pits on beaches all over the coast in the summer months, the brimming pot can be cooked on a home stove when the weather turns cold. Just find a large pan with a tight-fitting lid, some seaweed if possible (some markets give it out for free), and bring the beach to your kitchen.

Salt, to taste
8 small boiling onions, peeled
12 small red potatoes
2 pounds steamers
2 pounds mussels
4 ears fresh corn
Several pounds of rockweed (seaweed)
 or 2 tablespoons salt
4 lobsters (1 1/4 pounds each)
4 eggs (in their shells)
2 cups water
1/2 cup (1 stick) butter, melted
 (for serving)
2 lemons, cut into wedges (for serving)

1. Have on hand a 19-inch lobster pot with a tight-fitting lid or a 16-by-12-inch roasting pan and two layers of heavy-duty foil.
2. Bring a large saucepan of water to a boil. Add plenty of salt, and cook the onions and potatoes for 15 minutes or until they are tender when pierced with a skewer. Drain them.
3. Soak clams in cold water to remove their grit. Rinse the mussels with cold water and remove their beards by pulling them off from tip to hinge. Discard any mussels and clams with broken shells or that don't move when tapped. Remove the outer husks from the corn, pull out the silk, and leave the inner husks intact.
4. Add a layer of seaweed to the bottom of the pot or roasting pan. Lay the lobsters on the seaweed. Tuck the corn, whole eggs, and onions between the lobsters and the sides of the pan.
5. Place more seaweed over the lobsters. Add the mussels, clams, and potatoes. Cover with the remaining seaweed. Pour in the water.
6. Set the pot or roasting pan on your stovetop. Cover the pot or pan. (If using a roaster, make sure the foil is tucked securely under the top edge; place it across two burners.) Turn the heat to high. Start timing when you first see steam coming out of the edge. Cook for 15 minutes or until the clams open — you'll have to peek under the seaweed to check this — and the lobsters are bright red. Serve at once with melted butter, lemon wedges, and squares of cornbread.

☙ SARAH TOMLINSON
adapted from Great Eastern Mussel Farms in Maine

Lobster Pie

SERVES 4

Talk about gilding the lily: Lobster pie, also sometimes known as "lazy man's lobster," takes the summer seafood cake. Simmering the shelled flesh of the classic crustacean with cream, butter, and sherry brings out the sweet richness of lobster and turns what can be a late-summer staple into a dish fit for a king. At the Colonial-themed Publick House in Sturbridge, Massachusetts, the dish is a year-round staple, trailing only turkey in popularity.

TOPPING
1/2 cup dry white breadcrumbs
1/4 cup potato chips, crushed
1/4 cup grated Parmesan
1/4 teaspoon paprika
1 tablespoon dry sherry
2 tablespoons melted butter
1/8 teaspoon salt

In a bowl, combine the breadcrumbs, potato chips, Parmesan, paprika, sherry, butter, and salt. Stir well and set aside.

FILLING
Butter (for the dish)
1 pound cooked lobster meat
 (from about two 1 1/2-pound lobsters)
2 cups clam juice or fish stock
2 tablespoons unsalted butter
2 tablespoons flour
3 tablespoons dry sherry
1/2 teaspoon paprika
1/2 teaspoon tomato paste
1/2 cup heavy cream
Salt and white pepper, to taste

1. Set the oven at 350 degrees. Have on hand a 2-quart baking dish. Butter it. Fill it with the lobster meat.
2. In a large saucepan, bring the clam juice or fish stock to a boil; pour it into a bowl.
3. In the same saucepan, melt the butter. Whisk in the flour and cook over low heat, whisking constantly, for 2 minutes. Slowly whisk in the

hot clam juice or stock until the mixture is smooth. Add the sherry, paprika, tomato paste, and cream. Cook, whisking constantly, until the mixture comes to a boil. Season to taste with salt and white pepper. Lower the heat and simmer for 15 minutes.

4. Pour cream sauce over the lobster. Sprinkle with the crumb topping.

5. Bake the pie for 25 minutes or until the sauce is bubbling at the edges and the mixture is very hot.

❧ CLEA SIMON
adapted from the Publick House

Baked Stuffed Shrimp

Ⓢ Ⓔ Ⓡ Ⓥ Ⓔ Ⓢ ④

In New England, if you sprinkle fish with a crisp and flavorful cracker topping, or if you take that topping and press it onto the fish before you roll it up, you're making what is commonly known as "baked stuffed." Baked stuffed toppings are unbelievably rich, loaded with butter and garlic.

Osterville, Massachusetts, real estate agent Gerri Sullivan has been making a version of this shrimp recipe ever since she owned a Cape Cod restaurant some years ago.

Butter (for the pan)
4 ounces (1 sleeve) Ritz crackers, oyster crackers, or saltines

1/4 cup grated onion
1 clove garlic, chopped
6 ounces fresh crabmeat
2 tablespoons sherry
1/2 cup (1 stick) butter, melted
Ground pepper, to taste
1 1/2 pounds extra-large shrimp, peeled

1. Set the oven at 400 degrees. Have on hand a rimmed baking sheet; butter it lightly.

2. In the bowl of a food processor, work the crackers in on-off motions until they are finely chopped. Transfer to a bowl.

3. Add the onion and garlic to the processor bowl and work again just to combine them. Add the crabmeat and pulse to chop.

4. Return the cracker crumbs to the processor bowl. Add the sherry, melted butter, and pepper. Work in on-off motions just until the mixture holds together.

5. With the tip of a small knife, cut along the outside curve of the shrimp — not all the way through — to butterfly them. Open the shrimp and set them cut sides up on the baking sheet. Top each one with some stuffing mixture.

6. Bake the shrimp in the hot oven for 10 minutes or until they are cooked through.

❧ SHERYL JULIAN AND JULIE RIVEN
adapted from Gerri Sullivan of Osterville, Massachusetts

Sea Clam Pie

Ⓢ Ⓔ Ⓡ Ⓥ Ⓔ Ⓢ ⑥

In the mid-1800s, seawater was the lifeblood of Provincetown, Massachusetts, attracting large numbers of Portuguese fishermen and whalers.

Gradually, as Portuguese families began to settle in Provincetown, their food took its place alongside New England fare such as cod and baked beans.

Sea clams baked with linguica sausage and bread cubes, an old Portuguese dish, is perpetually on the menu at Clem & Ursie's Restaurant and Market in Provincetown.

2 tablespoons olive oil
1 large onion, chopped
2 cloves garlic, chopped
1/2 pound linguica, removed from casing and diced
1 quart chopped clams (thawed if frozen)
1 cup bread cubes
2 tablespoons clam broth, as necessary
1 baked 10-inch pie crust

1. Set the oven at 350 degrees.

2. In a large skillet over medium-high heat, heat the oil and cook the onions and garlic for 5 minutes or until the onions are soft. Add the linguica and cook, stirring, 5 minutes more.

3. Transfer the mixture into a large bowl and stir in the clams and bread cubes. If the mixture seems dry, add enough clam broth to moisten it. (Too much makes the crust gummy.) Spread the clam mixture in the pie crust, and return the pie to the oven. Continue baking it for 30 minutes or until the top is brown.

Note: You can also prepare this without the crust, as a casserole. Grease the 10-inch pie pan, spread the clam mixture in the pan, and bake for 30 minutes.

❧ ANDREA PYENSON
adapted from Clem & Ursie's

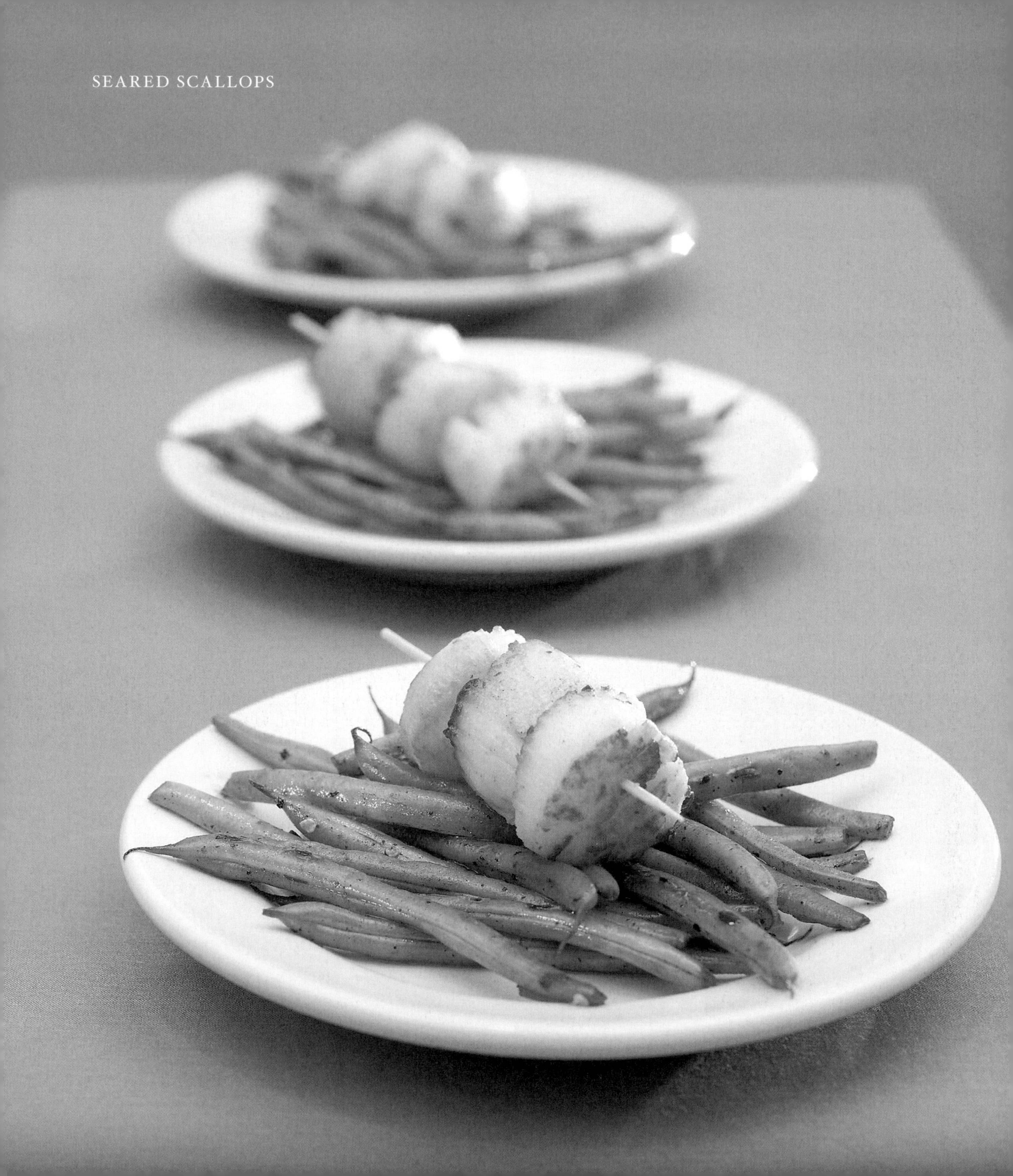

SEARED SCALLOPS

Seared Scallops with Spicy Green Beans

ⓈⒺⓇⓋⒺⓈ ④

One-pot meals suggest heavy dishes, meaty stews in wine, and all kinds of root vegetables. But the same system can be applied to seasonal greens and to lighter foods in general. The idea that you can make everything on one burner without turning on the oven will come in handy on hot summer nights or when you rent a beach house and there's only one pot on hand. Of course, if you're like us, you'll bring your favorite pot along with you.

3 tablespoons peanut oil
1 1/2 pounds sea scallops
Salt, to taste
1-inch piece fresh ginger, cut into slivers
1 clove garlic, finely chopped
1 or 2 dried red chili peppers, crumbled
1 1/2 pounds green beans, trimmed
1/2 cup water
2 tablespoons soy sauce
2 tablespoons seasoned rice vinegar
1/4 teaspoon sugar
8 9-inch wooden skewers

1. In a large heavy-based skillet, heat 2 tablespoons of the oil. Add the scallops and sprinkle them with salt. Sear the scallops over high heat for 1 1/2 minutes on a side or just until they are cooked on the outside, but not all the way through. Remove the scallops from the pan and transfer them to a plate. Set aside until you are ready to use them.

2. Without wiping out the skillet, heat the remaining 1 tablespoon of oil. Add the ginger, garlic, and chili peppers. Cook the mixture over medium heat, stirring constantly, for 30 seconds. Add the green beans and continue cooking, still stirring, for 2 minutes.

3. Add the water, soy sauce, vinegar, and sugar. Cover the pan and cook the beans for 1 minute more.

4. Meanwhile, thread the scallops on the skewers. Set the skewers on the green beans. Cover the pan and cook the beans and scallops for 2 minutes or until the scallops are cooked through and hot and the beans are tender.

5. Arrange the green beans on each of 4 dinner plates, add skewers to each plate, and serve at once

❦ SHERYL JULIAN AND JULIE RIVEN

Scallops Au Gratin

ⓈⒺⓇⓋⒺⓈ ④

There are few savory dishes that don't taste even better after you add a crusty topping. This technique goes by the French term "gratinee," which means that vegetables, fish, or pasta are dusted with breadcrumbs mixed with butter and grated cheese, then baked until the topping melts into the food and has a satisfying crunch and a golden color.

In the classic French dish coquilles St. Jacques au gratin, scallops are covered with a white-wine cream sauce and sprinkled with cheesy crumbs before baking. This is a variation on the classic.

Butter (for the dish)
1 1/2 pounds sea scallops
2 tablespoons unsalted butter
1/2 cup fresh, white breadcrumbs
1 clove garlic, finely chopped
1/3 cup heavy cream
2 tablespoons chopped fresh parsley
2 tablespoons freshly grated
   Parmesan cheese
Salt and pepper, to taste

1. Set the oven at 400 degrees. Have on hand a 10-inch-long baking dish or another dish that will hold the scallops in one layer. Butter the dish.

2. Remove and discard the small membrane on one side of each scallop. Place the scallops in the dish and cover loosely. Refrigerate.

3. In a heavy-based saucepan, melt the 2 tablespoons of butter and add the breadcrumbs and garlic. Cook over medium heat for 2 minutes or until the crumbs begin to change color. They should not cook until golden. Remove the pan from the heat and let the crumbs cool.

4. Take the scallops from the refrigerator. Spoon the cream over the scallops.

5. Stir the parsley, cheese, salt, and pepper into the crumb mixture and sprinkle the crumbs on the scallops.

6. Bake for 20 minutes or until the scallops are cooked through and the crumbs are golden. Serve at once.

❦ SHERYL JULIAN AND JULIE RIVEN

Eastern Halibut Braised in White Wine with Maine Shrimp SERVES 4

2-3 tablespoons canola oil
4 halibut fillets, 6 ounces each
Salt and white pepper
1/2 medium white onion,
  peeled and sliced thin
1/2 teaspoon chopped fresh thyme leaves
1 cup dry white wine
1/2 head escarole, outer leaves removed,
  cut into thin chiffonade ribbons
12 ounces Maine shrimp, peeled
4 tablespoons extra virgin olive oil
  or butter
1 teaspoon lemon juice

1. Set the oven at 350 degrees.
2. In a sauté pan large enough to hold the halibut fillets without crowding them, heat the canola oil over medium-high heat for two minutes.
3. Sprinkle the fillets with salt and pepper. Place them in the pan and brown on one side for about 3-4 minutes. Turn the fish over and add the sliced onions and thyme. Continue to cook for about 3 minutes.
4. Add the white wine and escarole and bring to a boil. Cover the pan and place in the oven. Cook the fish for about 6 minutes or until it is just cooked.
5. Remove the pan from the oven and remove the halibut to a warm platter.
6. Add the shrimp to the pan and cook over high heat for about 3 minutes. Add the olive oil or butter and the lemon juice and re-season with salt and pepper to taste. Cook over high heat for 1 minute, stirring to distribute the olive oil and lemon juice.
7. Spoon the shrimp mixture onto warm plates. Place the halibut on top. Serve with lemon wedges.

Y GORDON HAMERSLEY

GORDON HAMERSLEY
The chef-owner of Hamersley's Bistro started cooking as an undergrad at Boston University, then honed his skills in California and France before returning to the Hub. He won the James Beard Best Chef/Northeast award in 1995, and his first cookbook, "Bistro Cooking at Home" (Broadway), won the International Association of Culinary Professionals Cookbook Award in 2004.

"I love the way the sweet little Maine shrimp enhance the clean, briny taste of the Eastern halibut."

seafood hot pot

paella with mussels

shrimp and lemon risotto

pressed salmon sushi

linguine with clams

Pasta

When we think about seafood, our minds do not automatically go to pasta and rice. Sure, most of us are familiar with linguine and white clam sauce; many even know paella — specialties of Italy and Spain, respectively. That is how we expand our culinary horizons, taking local ingredients and using them in dishes that may not be synonymous with New England. Like sushi, or a seafood hot pot with Chinese noodles and Mongolian sauce. But there's nothing wrong with staying close to home, either. Tuna noodle casserole, anyone?

and Rice

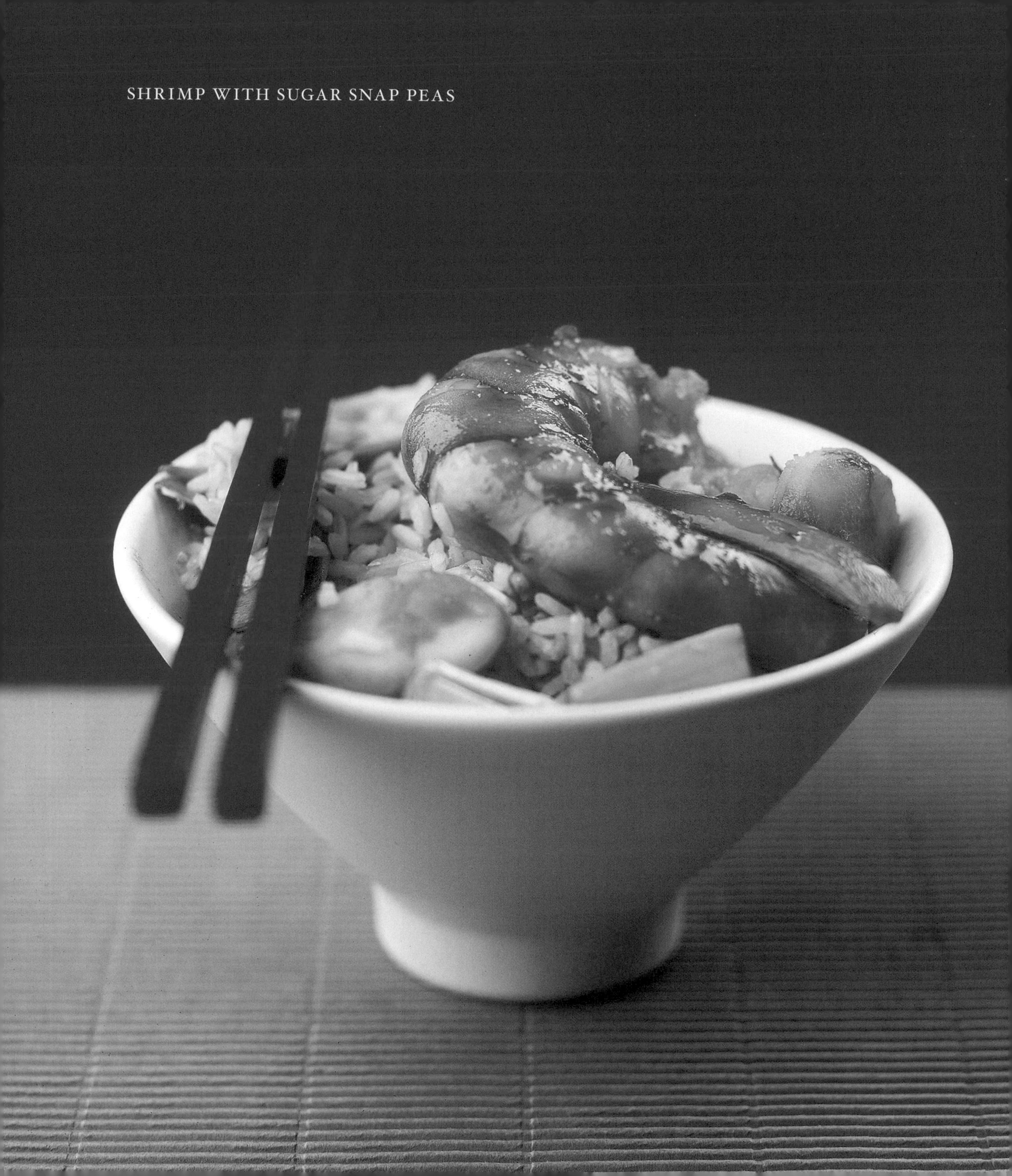

SHRIMP WITH SUGAR SNAP PEAS

Keep it Moving

🐟 BY SHERYL JULIAN, Globe Staff, and JULIE RIVEN, Globe Correspondent

Every cook knows how to make a stir-fry, because the name so completely describes what you do: You stir the food as it fries in the pan. If you have all the ingredients beside you at the stove, the dish takes minutes, and you sit down to a nutritious and satisfying supper that has crunch and great texture.

Stir-fries can be tossed in a wok, which Chinese cooks have been using for centuries, or you can use a big, heavy skillet. In either case, you need lots of heat, which can smoke up the kitchen if there's no ventilation hood.

The idea behind the stir-fry technique is to cook the food as quickly as possible. Once the food goes into the pan, keep it moving so that all sides of each morsel hit the heat.

Although Asian cooks mostly use white rice for stir-fries, we prefer brown rice, which has more nutrients and is chewier than the white varieties. Brown rice is one of those dishes that mystifies cooks, but it's made the same way as any other rice. You just need to know how much water per cup of rice to use. Try it several times until you get it right with the kind of brown rice you buy.

Shrimp with Sugar Snap Peas

SERVES 4

2 tablespoons peanut oil
1/2 pound sugar snap peas,
    trimmed and strings removed
1/2 cup thinly sliced water chestnuts
4 scallions, trimmed and cut
    into 1/2-inch pieces
1 clove garlic, chopped
1 pound large shrimp,
    shelled and deveined
1 tablespoon chili sauce with garlic
2 tablespoons seasoned rice wine vinegar
2 tablespoons soy sauce
1/2 cup chicken stock
1 recipe brown rice

1. In a wok or large skillet, heat 1 tablespoon of the oil. Add the sugar snap peas, water chestnuts, and scallions. Stir-fry over high heat for 2 minutes.
2. Add the garlic and cook, stirring, for 30 seconds. With a slotted spoon, remove the vegetables from the pan.
3. Without wiping out the pan, add the remaining 1 tablespoon of oil. Add the shrimp and stir-fry over high heat for 3 minutes or until the shrimp are pink and cooked through.
4. Remove the shrimp from the pan with a slotted spoon.
5. Add the chili sauce, rice vinegar, soy sauce, and stock. Cook over high heat for 1 minute.
6. Return the shrimp and vegetables to the pan and cook for 30 seconds or until they are hot.
7. Spoon the rice into 4 bowls, add the shrimp mixture, and serve at once.
🍸 SHERYL JULIAN AND JULIE RIVEN

Brown Rice

SERVES 4

2 1/2 cups water
1/2 teaspoon salt
1 cup long-grain brown rice

1. In a saucepan, bring the water and salt to a boil. Add the rice and when the water returns to a boil, turn the heat to low.
2. Cover the pan and cook the rice for 45 to 50 minutes or until it is tender when tasted.
3. Leave the cover on the pan and set aside for 10 minutes before serving. Fluff with a fork.
🍸 SHERYL JULIAN AND JULIE RIVEN

We Dig Linguine

🐟 BY KERI FISHER, Globe Correspondent

Wet sand under your feet, a whiff of salt sea air, a stretch of beach at sunrise as your vista — clamming is a feast of the senses even before you pry one open.

As if that isn't enough enticement to roll up your pantlegs and start digging, there's more: "There is no chance of failing," says Christopher Reaske, author of "The Compleat Clammer." "If you do some homework in advance, you will have delicious rewards."

The first requirement is a recreational shellfishing permit, available at town hall in each seaside town. Shellfish wardens patrol beaches, checking for licenses.

Regulations vary according to each town and state in New England. Most licenses come with a pamphlet on the local rules and a map showing the areas where you can shellfish.

Regulations also govern the minimum size you can dig — usually one inch wide for hard-shelled clams, two inches long for mussels and soft-shelled clams. You are also subject to stay within other boundaries: amounts you can harvest each day or week, areas in which you can dig, the season for shellfishing, and what tools you can use.

If you're digging for soft-shell clams, known as steamers, you'll need a short-handled rake. For hard-shell clams, known as quahogs, or chowder clams (the largest ones), cherrystones, and littlenecks, you'll need a long-handled rake. You'll also need a gauge, to make sure your catch meets the minimum size requirements, and at least one basket, to carry your bounty.

Shellfishing truly brings out the little kid inside. To find clams, look for small, uniform holes on the surface of the sand. These holes are caused when clams expel water. Often you may even see water squirting right out of the sand. That's a dead giveaway that clams are close by.

Oval holes indicate razor

clams, larger holes indicate steamers, and tiny holes indicate quahogs. Use your rake to dig into the sand and find your catch. Steamers live about one foot beneath the surface, quahogs often less than six inches. Razor clams are close to the surface but very fast — once you dig up some earth, be prepared to grab them quickly.

Mussels can be found simply hanging out in clusters along the shore, usually attached to each other and probably a rock. Mussels use fine, sinewy strands, called beards, to attach themselves; be sure to remove these beards before eating. Often these wild mussels will be covered with barnacles, which are only an aesthetic fault. Chip them off with a rock.

There is something magical about being out on the ocean at dawn, sifting through the damp earth for mollusks. "The best part," says Reaske, "is that you can have a great encounter with the natural world at virtually no cost and still conclude the encounter with some delicious dinner fare."

And really, it all comes down to good eating.

Linguine with White Clam Sauce
ⓢⓔⓡⓥⓔⓢ ④

You can use whatever clams you dig up — larger clams, shucked and chopped, for the sauce and smaller clams, in their shells, for garnish. The amounts of each are simply guidelines. Use what you dig.

16 cherrystone clams
Salt and black pepper, to taste
1 pound (1 box) linguine
4 tablespoons olive oil
16 littleneck clams
1/4 teaspoon crushed red pepper
4 anchovy fillets, chopped
3 medium tomatoes, coarsely chopped

3 tablespoons chopped garlic
2 tablespoons chopped parsley
1 cup reserved clam juice
1 tablespoon chopped fresh thyme
2 tablespoons chopped fresh basil

1. Over a bowl, shuck the cherrystones, dropping the clams into the juice as they are opened. Discard the shells. Gently swirl the clams in the juice to rinse them. Lift the clams out of the juice and chop them coarsely. Refrigerate the clams until ready to use.

2. Add enough water to the clam juice to increase the volume by half. Let the juices sit about five minutes. Slowly pour off 1 cup of juice, leaving any sediment or sludge in the bowl. Discard the sludge and the remaining juice.

3. Bring a large pan of salted water to a boil, drop in the linguine, and let it cook in rapidly boiling water, stirring once or twice, for 6 minutes or until the pasta is tender but still has some bite.

4. Meanwhile, prepare the clams: In a large skillet over high heat, heat 2 tablespoons of the oil. When it is hot, add the littlenecks, crushed red pepper, and anchovies. Cover the pan and check it after 1 minute. When the littlenecks start to open, add the chopped clams, tomatoes, garlic, parsley, and reserved clam juice.

5. Bring to a boil and simmer for 5 minutes. Remove the pan from the heat, pour in the remaining 2 tablespoons olive oil, thyme, basil, salt, and black pepper.

6. Drain the linguine and transfer it to a bowl. Pour over the clam mixture, toss to combine, and divide the linguine among 4 pasta bowls, giving each person some of the littlenecks. Serve at once.

🍸 KERI FISHER

Seafood Hot Pot
ⓢⓔⓡⓥⓔⓢ ⑥

Dipping into a community pot at the dinner table encourages participants to become instantly intimate. You have to sit closely, and no matter how careful you are, the sauce drips. The whole enterprise turns into fun. Mongolian hot pots use flavorful broths for dipping meat and vegetables; the Japanese shabu-shabu is a similar pot of broth; and Italians who live near the French and Swiss Alps make a warm, aromatic bath of oil for dipping vegetables. All of these dishes require a table burner, which should be steady enough to hold hot liquid without tipping. Begin the cooking in the kitchen and then transfer the dipping mixture to a heatproof bowl to keep warm over a burner on the table.

1/2 pound medium shrimp, peeled
1/2 pound scallops
1 pound firm-fleshed white fish fillets, such as haddock or halibut, cut into 1-inch pieces
1/2 cup Chinese rice wine or sake
1-inch piece fresh ginger, chopped
1 1/2 teaspoons toasted sesame oil
1 teaspoon peanut oil
4 cloves garlic, lightly smashed
1 small Napa cabbage, cut into 2-inch squares, stem and tender leafy sections separated
5 cups chicken broth

Salt, to taste
1/2 pound flat Chinese wheat noodles or
other flat noodles, cooked in boiling
water for 2 minutes or until tender
2 tablespoons finely chopped
scallion greens

1. In three serving bowls, place the shrimp, scallops, and fish; set aside.
2. In a small bowl, whisk together 1/4 cup of the rice wine or sake and the ginger and sesame oil. Divide the marinade among the three bowls of seafood. Toss each and refrigerate.
3. Place a large flameproof casserole over high heat. Add the peanut oil and heat for 30 seconds or until it is almost smoking. Add the garlic and cabbage stems and stir-fry for 1 minute or until the cabbage is slightly limp. Add the remaining 1/4 cup rice wine, toss the cabbage lightly, and cover the pan. Cook for 1 1/2 minutes.
4. Add the cabbage leaves and the chicken broth to the casserole. Bring to a boil, lower the heat, and simmer for 30 minutes. Add a generous pinch of salt.
5. Remove the pot and set it on a burner at the table. Bring the 3 bowls of seafood to the table. Have the guests skewer the seafood and hold it in the simmering broth until it is cooked through.
6. Divide the cooked noodles among six soup bowls. Spoon the soup and

cabbage over the noodles and top with the seafood. Sprinkle with scallions and serve with Mongolian sauce.

MONGOLIAN SAUCE
3/4 cup soy sauce
3 1/2 tablespoons Chinese rice wine
or sake
3 1/2 tablespoons Chinese black vinegar
or Worcestershire sauce
3 tablespoons finely chopped scallions
2 tablespoons finely chopped ginger
2 tablespoons finely chopped garlic
2 tablespoons sugar
1 teaspoon hot chili paste (optional)

In a bowl, combine the soy sauce, rice wine or sake, black vinegar or Worcestershire sauce, scallions, ginger, garlic, sugar, and chili paste, if using. Set the mixture aside. (It will keep, refrigerated, for up to 1 week).

☙ SHERYL JULIAN AND JULIE RIVEN
adapted from Nina Simonds's "Asian Noodles: 75 Dishes to Twirl, Slurp, and Savor" (Hearst Books)

Spaghetti al Sugo di Aragosta
SERVES 2

For his magisterial cookbook, "A Mediterranean Feast," Clifford Wright borrowed this recipe from the Fantasia family, owners of New Deal Fish Market in Cambridge,

Massachusetts. The lobster tail can be reserved for stuffing and roasting, making a perfect second course. If you are squeamish about killing a lobster, you can buy a cooked one in many supermarkets and lobster pounds.

1 live lobster, 1 1/2 to 2 pounds
3 tablespoons olive oil
1 small red bell pepper, minced
3-5 tablespoons minced parsley
3 cloves garlic, minced
1 28-ounce can whole tomatoes,
broken into pieces by hand
Salt
1/2 pound spaghetti

1. Swiftly cut the live lobster down the middle, lengthwise, and remove the gray head sac just behind the eyes. Cut off and reserve the claws and the tail. Save all the juice.
2. Sauté the cut-up lobster in a large pan in the olive oil with the red pepper, parsley, and garlic. Cover and cook over medium-high heat for 10 minutes, until the lobster is red.
3. Add the tomatoes and salt to taste. Simmer for 45 minutes, covered. Remove the cover near the end to firm up the sauce.
4. Meanwhile, boil the spaghetti in lots of salted water, until al dente. Toss with the sauce.

☙ TED WEESNER JR.
adapted from Clifford Wright's "A Mediterranean Feast" (Morrow)

To find clams at the beach, look for small, uniform holes on the surface of the sand. Often you may even see water squirting right out of the sand. That's a dead giveaway that clams are close by.

Skillet Fish and Rice

SERVES 4

Karyl Bannister of Southport, Maine, started writing her folksy "Cook & Tell" newsletter more than two decades ago. From her mother-in-law, Barbara Webster Shenton, comes this seafood rice dish, concocted while summering in an apartment perched on pilings in Gloucester, Massachusetts.

4 slices bacon
1 1/2 cups uncooked long-grain white rice
1 1/2 cups bottled clam juice
1 cup water
1/2 teaspoon salt
4 flounder or sole fillets
1 orange, thinly sliced

1. In a large cast-iron or other heavy skillet, render the bacon until it is crisp. Drain it and set it aside. Remove all but 2 tablespoons fat from the skillet.

2. Add the rice and cook over medium heat for 3 minutes, or until the rice grains are translucent. Add the clam juice, water, and salt.

3. Put the fillets on top, skinned side down, cover the skillet, and simmer the mixture for 20 minutes, or until the rice is just tender and the fish is cooked through. There's no need to stir the dish.

4. Arrange the orange slices around the edge of the skillet, crumble the bacon over the top, and serve from the skillet.

❧ SHERYL JULIAN AND JULIE RIVEN
adapted from Karyl Bannister's "Cook & Tell" (Houghton Mifflin)

Tuna Noodle Casserole with Fresh Mushrooms

SERVES 4-6

All of us whose mothers ever pulled a pan of creamy tuna noodle casserole from the oven can attest to its warming qualities. The standard recipe of canned tuna, cream of mushroom soup, and frozen peas is as much the definition of American comfort food as meatloaf or mashed potatoes. As is true of meatloaf, part of the craving is the signature twist on the dish from your childhood home, whether it had toasted breadcrumbs or a crushed potato chip topping, without which, it just isn't right.

8 ounces pasta, such as rotini
  or egg noodles
2 6-ounce cans tuna, well drained
1 tablespoon butter
1 small onion, chopped
1 small green pepper, chopped
2 cups fresh button mushrooms, sliced
1/2 cup fresh breadcrumbs
Butter for topping
3 tablespoons butter
1 tablespoon cornstarch
2 cups milk (lowfat is fine)
1/2 cup fresh Parmesan cheese, grated
1 tablespoon Dijon mustard

1. Cook pasta according to package directions, until al dente. Rinse in cold water, drain well, and set aside in a lightly greased 8-inch square glass baking dish or round ceramic casserole dish.

2. Use a fork to flake the tuna out of the can and onto the noodles.

3. Set the oven at 350 degrees.

4. Melt 1 tablespoon butter in nonstick saucepan. Add onion, and cook 1 minute before adding the pepper and mushrooms. Sauté mushrooms until tender, about 5 minutes. Spoon sautéed vegetables onto noodles.

5. In the same saucepan, make the sauce; melt 3 tablespoons butter. Stir in cornstarch to form a paste. Gradually stir in milk. Bring to a boil over medium heat and boil for 3 minutes, stirring constantly, or until thickened. Add cheese and mustard, and cook until cheese melts. Remove from heat and pour over casserole, mixing gently to coat.

6. Sprinkle with breadcrumbs, and dot lightly with butter. Bake for 30 minutes, or until bubbling.

❧ SARAH TOMLINSON
adapted from Maryana Vollstedt's "The Big Book of Casseroles" (Chronicle Books)

The standard Tuna Noodle Casserole recipe of canned tuna, mushroom soup, and frozen peas is as much the definition of comfort food as meatloaf.

Shrimp and Lemon Risotto

S E R V E S   4

1 pound medium shrimp
1 lemon
2 tablespoons pure olive oil
1 medium onion, chopped into
  1/4-inch dice
1 1/2 cups Arborio rice
2 garlic cloves, minced
1 cup clam juice
4 cups chicken stock or high-quality
  low-sodium canned chicken broth
2 tablespoons chopped fresh flat-leaf
  parsley (optional)

1. Peel and devein the shrimp; refrigerate until ready to use.
2. Wash the lemon and use a vegetable peeler or paring knife to remove a strip of zest (the yellow part of the rind) about half an inch wide. Slice this into julienned strips as narrow as you can manage. Cover and set aside.
3. Grate the remaining yellow part of the rind. Cover and set aside (it dries out quickly). Squeeze the juice from the lemon and set aside.
4. Heat the olive oil over medium heat in the pressure cooker. Add the onion and cook until it turns translucent, 3 to 5 minutes, stirring constantly. The bottom of a pressure cooker is not as thick as a heavy sauté pan or casserole so you need to be vigilant so the onion doesn't burn.
5. Stir in the rice and cook until it just starts to toast, a couple of minutes. Add the garlic, still stirring, and cook until it becomes aromatic,

only a minute. Add the clam juice and 2 cups of chicken stock.
6. Lock the lid in place, increase the heat to high and bring the pot to high pressure. Adjust the heat to maintain the high pressure for 5 minutes.
7. While the rice is cooking, bring the remaining 2 cups of stock to a simmer.
8. After 5 minutes, remove the pressure cooker from heat, use the quick release method to lower the pressure, and remove the lid. Return the pot to the stove. The risotto should still be a little underdone. With the pressure cooker over medium heat, stir in additional warm stock, one ladle at a time, waiting until each addition is absorbed before adding more.
9. When the risotto reaches the proper texture (it should taste cooked, but the grains should offer a hint of resistance), add half the lemon juice and all the lemon zest.
10. Carefully stir the shrimp into the risotto, adding more stock if the risotto seems too thick. They will only take a couple of minutes to cook.
11. Adjust the seasonings, adding more lemon juice or salt, if necessary. Serve the risotto on warmed plates or in warmed bowls, garnishing each portion with strips of lemon zest and parsley.
Note: A heat diffuser under the pot will keep the thick sauce from forming a crust on the bottom of the pan.

❧ KEN RIVARD
adapted from Lorna Sass's "Cooking Under Pressure" (HarperCollins)

GADGETS

Rice Cookers

Perfectly made or even well-made rice takes practice and care, and rice cookers promise to take all that thinking out of the process. Add the grains and the liquid, turn the thing on, and it automatically cooks the rice until it senses that the moisture has been absorbed; then it switches to a mode that will keep the rice warm for many hours. That's the most basic approach, anyway. Companies now make rice cookers that will steam food while the rice is cooking, or even double as a slow cooker, a la Crock Pot.

Ultimately, the question of whether to buy a rice cooker is a matter of priorities. If you make rice only periodically, or you want to master the subtleties of a world of varieties, then you're probably better off staying with the stovetop method. But if you just want basic rice on the table quickly and easily, day in and day out, a rice cooker might be worth the price, and the counter space.

When I tested five cookers, two stood out. An inexpensive one by **Rival** (www.rivalproducts.com) is simple to operate, and in my testing produced beautifully fluffy long-grain white rice and brown rice, but overcooked Japanese-style medium-grain rice. A much more expensive **Sanyo** cooker (store.sanyousa.com) with micro-computerized controls was very slow, but it made close to perfect rice across the board.

❧ JOE YONAN

Spaghetti with Shrimp and Artichokes

S E R V E S 4

1 tablespoon olive oil
2 cloves garlic
1 can (1 pound) imported tomatoes, crushed in a bowl
1/4 teaspoon sugar
1 pound spaghetti
1 1/2 cups spaghetti cooking liquid
1/2 pound medium shrimp, peeled
1 package (10-12 ounces) frozen artichoke hearts, boiled 5 minutes and drained
1/4 pound imported feta cheese
3 tablespoons fresh oregano
1/4 cup chopped black olives
Salt and pepper, to taste

1. In a skillet, heat the oil and cook the garlic for 30 seconds. Add the tomatoes and sugar. Bring them to a boil. Let them bubble steadily for 5 minutes. Set the pan aside.
2. Bring a large pot of salted water to a boil and add the spaghetti. Stir until the water returns to a boil and let the pasta bubble steadily for 8 minutes or until it is tender but still has some bite. Before you drain the spaghetti, dip a heatproof 2-cup measuring cup into the pot and remove 1 1/2 cups of cooking liquid.
3. Drain the pasta and return it to the pot with 1/2 cup of the cooking liquid. Cover the pot and set it aside.
4. Add the remaining 1 cup of cooking liquid to the tomatoes and bring to a boil. Add the shrimp and artichoke hearts and cook for 2 minutes or until both shrimp and artichokes

are cooked through.
5. Pour the sauce over the spaghetti and toss thoroughly. Add the feta, oregano, olives, salt, and pepper and toss again. Serve at once.

❦ SHERYL JULIAN AND JULIE RIVEN

Salmon Kedgeree

S E R V E S 8

Kedgeree is a popular English breakfast and lunch dish. It was adapted by the British from an Indian curry recipe. In England, kedgeree is often made with smoked haddock; salmon makes the dish dressier.

Salt and pepper, to taste
2 cups long-grain white rice
4 eggs
1/2 cup (1 stick) unsalted butter
1 1/2 tablespoons curry powder
2 cups heavy cream
1 recipe roasted salmon (see recipe)
3 tablespoons chopped fresh parsley

1. Bring 3 1/2 quarts of salted water to a boil in a large saucepan. Sprinkle the rice into the water and let the water return to a boil. Cook the rice, stirring occasionally, for 12 minutes exactly (it will not absorb the water).
2. Drain the rice into a colander. Use the handle of a wooden spoon to poke 6 holes in the rice; set it aside for 10 minutes.
3. Bring another saucepan of water to a boil. With a straight pin or safety pin, poke a hole in the rounded end of each egg. Gently lower them into the boiling water and, when the water returns to a boil, cook the eggs

for 10 minutes exactly. Transfer the eggs to a bowl of ice water. Use the back of a spoon to crack the shells all over and peel off a strip of shell (this makes the eggs cool faster in the water). When the eggs are cold, peel them and leave them in the cold water.
4. In a large flameproof casserole, melt the butter and stir in the curry powder. Cook for 1 minute. Add the rice and cook, stirring, for a few minutes or until the rice is completely covered with curry powder. Add the cream, salt, and pepper and heat gently just to warm the cream.
5. Add the salmon and cook over low heat for a few minutes until the mixture is hot. Spoon the salmon and rice onto a large platter. Dry the eggs with paper towels and quarter them. Arrange them around the kedgeree. Sprinkle with parsley.

❦ SHERYL JULIAN AND JULIE RIVEN

Roasted Salmon

S E R V E S 6

2 pounds skinless, boneless salmon
Vegetable oil (for sprinkling)
Salt and pepper, to taste

1. Set the oven at 450 degrees. Lay the salmon on a baking dish, boned side up. Rub it with oil, salt, and pepper. Press a piece of parchment paper directly onto the salmon and set it in the hot oven.
2. Roast the salmon for 15 minutes or until it is cooked through but still moist. Set the salmon aside until cool, then flake it into 2-inch pieces.

❦ SHERYL JULIAN AND JULIE RIVEN

SALMON KEDGEREE

Hard-boiled eggs and marinated red onions complement the popular British dish kedgeree, dressed up here with roasted salmon.

Making Sushi Fun ~ BY DEBRA SAMUELS, Globe Correspondent

Making sushi at home may seem fussy and complicated, but it doesn't have to be.

Sushi is not raw fish. It is the sweet and vinegary rice that forms the base for raw or cooked fish, vegetables, and a variety of toppings. A dollop of sushi rice is placed atop a rectangle of yaki nori (roasted seaweed). Then one chooses from a kaleidoscope of foods and places them on the rice. The seaweed and rice combination can then be rolled, cone-like, and lightly dipped in soy sauce.

Excellent ingredients are important, as they will be standing on their own merits. Raw fish must be bought at reputable places. If you don't like raw fish, use smoked salmon, or cooked crabmeat and shrimp. Cucumber strips, radish sprouts, watercress, shiso leaves, avocados, steamed asparagus, sweet shiitake mushrooms, and omelet strips provide balance and texture. Cutting things into similar sizes and grouping them on a large platter makes a beautiful presentation. Condiments are soy sauce, wasabi, and vinegared ginger slices.

Rice remains the most important ingredient. There is no substitute for short-grain, Japanese rice. Its "sticky" characteristic gives it the distinctive quality necessary in making sushi. Short-grain rice must be washed and soaked before cooking, and the water must be cold when the rice begins to cook. After cooking, a mixture of rice wine vinegar, sugar, and salt is stirred into the steaming rice, coating the grains until shiny.

Most of the makings of a sushi party can be found in any supermarket with a reasonable international or Asian section. You can make all the sushi for your party yourself, or give everyone an assignment. Green tea (available in tea bags), Japanese beer, and hot sake are traditional accompanying drinks.

Pressed Salmon Sushi

MAKES 30 PIECES

Known as oshizushi, these pressed sushi pieces are served on a platter sprinkled with scallions. To dip the pieces in soy sauce, turn them salmon side down; if you dip the rice end first, the pieces fall apart.

RICE

2 1/2 cups short-grain white rice
2 3/4 cups water
5 tablespoons rice wine vinegar
2 tablespoons sugar
1/2 teaspoon salt

1. In a bowl, place the rice and enough water to cover it. Wash the rice by stirring it and draining it. Do this three more times or until the water becomes almost clear. Let the rice soak for 20 minutes.
2. In a pot, combine the rice and 2 3/4 cups water. Bring to a boil over medium heat. Cover and cook for 5 minutes. Turn the heat to low and cook 10 minutes more. Turn the heat off and let the rice steam for 10 minutes.
3. In a saucepan, combine the vinegar, sugar, and salt. Stir over low heat until the sugar and salt dissolve.
4. Transfer the rice to a large bowl. With large cutting movements, use a wooden spoon to toss the rice without mashing it. Sprinkle the vinegar mixture onto the rice as you toss to coat the grains. Fan the rice to cool it as you mix it. Cover with a clean, damp dish towel.

TOPPING

3/4 cup mayonnaise
2 teaspoons liquid hot sauce
Dash of cayenne pepper
1 teaspoon dark sesame oil
2 cups arugula leaves
12 ounces smoked salmon
3 scallions, finely chopped
Soy sauce (for dipping)

1. Set a 9-by-13-inch pan on the counter. Line the bottom with 2 pieces of plastic wrap, letting 8 inches hang over all sides. With moist hands, place half the sushi rice in the bottom of the pan. Press lightly to make a smooth layer.
2. In a bowl, stir together the mayonnaise, hot sauce, cayenne, and sesame oil. Spread half the mayonnaise mixture on the rice.
3. Add half the arugula and half the salmon slices.
4. Repeat with the remaining rice, mayonnaise mixture, arugula, and salmon. Fold the extra plastic wrap over the top layer. Place a large book on top and gently apply pressure. Set aside for 15 minutes to 1 hour.
5. Open the plastic wrap and use it to lift out the sushi. Set it on a cutting board. With a wet paper towel, moisten the edge of a sharp knife. Cut sushi into pieces about 1 by 2 inches each. Sprinkle with scallions. Serve with soy sauce.

— DEBRA SAMUELS

PRESSED SALMON SUSHI

Excellent ingredients are important, as they will be standing on their own merits. Raw fish must be bought at reputable places.

Classic Paella

SERVES 4

Contrary to popular belief, traditional Spanish paella does not mix meats and seafood. This paella depends on mussel meat for most of its flavor. The crust of rice on the bottom of the pan, called soccarat, is considered a delicacy in Spain. Even with the long list of ingredients, the dish is not difficult.

2 pounds mussels, cleaned
1/2 cup dry white wine
2 1/2 cups bottled clam juice
1/3 teaspoon crumbled saffron threads
2 eggs, hard-cooked and peeled
1/4 cup olive oil
1/2 pound medium shrimp, peeled
2 cloves garlic, chopped
1 onion, chopped
1 green bell pepper, chopped
1 tablespoon chopped
*   fresh rosemary leaves*
1/2 teaspoon salt
1 tomato, finely chopped
1 tablespoon chopped parsley
1/4 teaspoon paprika
*   (preferably pimenton)*
1 1/2 cups Spanish or
*   Arborio short-grain rice*
2 scallions, chopped
12 sugar snap peas, strings removed
1 canned pimiento, cut into strips

1. Set aside 16 of the mussels. Pour the wine into a large skillet, add the remaining mussels, cover, and cook over high heat for 5 to 7 minutes or until the mussels open.
2. Tip the cooking broth into a 4-cup measuring cup. Add enough clam juice to make 3 cups. Return the broth to the skillet. Add the saffron, and warm over low heat.
4. Remove the mussel meat from the open shells; chop it coarsely.
5. Set the oven at 400 degrees. Coarsely chop half of one egg; set aside. Slice the remaining 1 1/2 eggs for garnish.
5. In a large paella pan or cast-iron skillet, heat the oil over high heat. Add the shrimp and cook, stirring constantly, for 1 minute. Remove from the pan. Add the garlic, onion, green pepper, 1 1/2 teaspoons of the rosemary, and salt. Lower the heat to medium and cook the mixture for 3 minutes. Add the tomato and parsley and cook for 1 minute.
6. Stir in the paprika and rice until the grains are coated all over.
7. Pour in the hot broth, bring to a boil, and boil for about 2 minutes, stirring. Taste for salt and add the shrimp, chopped egg, and scallions. Continue to boil, stirring occasionally and rotating the pan if it is too big for one burner, for 3 minutes more or until the rice isn't soupy but sufficient liquid remains. Stir in the peas and set the pimiento and whole mussels on top.
8. Transfer the pan to the oven and cook for 10 to 12 minutes or until the rice is almost tender. Transfer to a warm spot, scatter with the sliced egg and the remaining rosemary, and let the paella sit for 5 to 10 minutes.
9. Return the pan to a burner and cook over high heat for 2 to 3 minutes, rotating the pan to evenly crisp the bottom of the rice.

▼ JOE YONAN
adapted from Penelope Casas's "Paella: Spectacular Rice Dishes From Spain" (Henry Holt and Co.)

Paella with Chicken, Mussels, and Shrimp

SERVES 6

With their crimson flesh and slightly sour taste, blood oranges add an exotic, mildly tart taste to cooked dishes, along with a tint of maroon that stains the food luxuriously. In a quick paella, combine tomatoes, which sweeten the dish, with sections of orange and a pinch of saffron, and your bowl of chicken, mussels, and shrimp is full of character. Instead of adding rice to the chicken and seafood, cook saffron rice separately.

8 chicken thighs, skin removed
Olive oil (for sprinkling)
Salt and black pepper, to taste
1 tablespoon olive oil
1 Spanish onion, coarsely chopped
1 clove garlic, finely chopped
1 cup canned imported tomatoes,
*   crushed in a bowl*
1 cup chicken stock
1 blood or navel orange, rind and pith
*   removed, flesh cut into 2-inch pieces*
1 teaspoon dried oregano
1/2 teaspoon crushed red pepper
Pinch of saffron
1/4 cup water
2 pounds mussels
1/2 pound large shrimp, peeled
2 tablespoons chopped fresh parsley

1. Set the oven at 400 degrees. Place the thighs, skinned side up, in a baking dish. Sprinkle with oil, salt, and black pepper. Roast the

chicken for 30 minutes or until the thighs are cooked through.

2. Meanwhile, in a large flameproof casserole, heat the oil and cook the onion with salt and black pepper over medium heat, stirring often, for 10 minutes or until the onion softens. Add the garlic and cook, stirring, for 30 seconds. Stir in the tomatoes, stock, oranges, oregano, crushed pepper, and saffron. Bring to a boil, lower the heat, and simmer for 10 minutes.

3. In a large saucepan with a tight-fitting lid, combine the water and mussels. Cover with the lid and set the pan over high heat. Bring the liquid to a boil and cook the mussels, shaking the pot once or twice, until the mussels open. Discard any that do not open. With a slotted spoon, lift the shellfish from the pot and transfer them to a bowl.

4. Line a strainer with several layers of cheesecloth. Strain the

shellfish broth into the tomato-and orange mixture. Add the chicken thighs and bring the mixture to a boil. Add the shrimp, submerging them in the liquid.

5. Cook the shrimp for 2 minutes, stirring gently, or until they are pink and firm. Add the mussels to the pot, sprinkle with parsley, and serve at once with saffron rice.

❧ SHERYL JULIAN AND JULIE RIVEN

Saffron Rice

SERVES 6

1 1/2 cups long-grain white rice
2 tablespoons vegetable oil
1 small onion, chopped
Salt and pepper, to taste
1/2 teaspoon saffron threads mixed with
    1/4 cup boiling water
3 cups chicken stock

1. In a large bowl of cold water, briefly stir the rice with your hand.

Tip it into a strainer.

2. In a large, heavy-based saucepan, heat the oil and cook the onion with a generous pinch of salt and pepper over medium heat, stirring occasionally, for 8 minutes or until the onion softens.

3. Add the saffron and its liquid and stir for 1 minute. Add the rice and stir well to coat the grains all over with the saffron mixture.

4. Pour in the stock, bring to a boil, lower the heat, and cover the pan. Simmer the rice for 18 minutes or until it is tender when you taste a few grains.

5. Remove the rice from the heat, let the pan sit for 8 to 10 minutes, then fluff the grains with a fork before serving.

❧ SHERYL JULIAN AND JULIE RIVEN

Penne with Braised Octopus and Tomato Sauce

SERVES 4

Forget any comparisons with the octopus that shows up on sushi platters (chewy and mildly acidic). Prepared using a pressure cooker, octopus in a tomato sauce with pasta is sweet and fork-tender. A few places carry fresh octopus regularly, but many supermarkets also carry it frozen, like icy softballs packaged in plastic wrap. Freezing has no affect on the flavor of octopus — simply thaw the octopus in a bowl of cold water before using — and it guarantees that the octopus has been cleaned already. If using baby octopus, leave the tentacles whole. In a pinch, you can substitute plain water for the chicken stock, clam juice, and white wine and still produce a flavorful stock. It just won't be as rich.

*2 pounds thawed octopus, cleaned
    (almost always sold this way)*
*1 cup chicken stock or high-quality,
    low-sodium canned chicken broth
    or water*
1 cup clam juice or water
1 cup dry white wine
1 teaspoon dried thyme
Kosher salt
1/4 cup extra virgin olive oil

*1 medium onion, chopped into
   half-inch dice*
3 cloves garlic, minced
*1 28-ounce can whole peeled tomatoes
   in tomato puree*
*Small pinch of hot red pepper flakes
   (optional)*
1 pound dried penne
*2 tablespoons chopped fresh flat-leaf
   parsley (optional)*

1. In a large pot, bring to a boil enough water to cover the octopus. Blanch the octopus in the boiling water for 5 minutes. Drain and let cool. The octopus now will be firm enough to cut into pieces.
2. Cut the head off just above the eyes. Discard the head. Cut the tentacles off the body. Slice the body and tentacles into 2-inch sections.
3. Place the octopus in a pressure cooker. Add the chicken stock, clam juice, and wine, and then add enough water to cover the octopus by a couple of inches. Add the thyme and 1 teaspoon of salt.
4. Lock the lid into place, bring the cooker to high pressure, and cook for 15 minutes, adjusting the heat as necessary to maintain the high pressure.
5. While the octopus is cooking, bring a large pot of salted water to a boil.
6. Heat the olive oil in a large, heavy-bottomed sauté pan. Add the onion, season with salt, and cook over medium heat until the onions have softened and turned translucent, five to seven minutes. Remove the pan from the heat and wait until the octopus finishes cooking before going any further.

7. After 15 minutes (10 minutes, if cooking baby octopus), remove the pressure cooker from the heat, use the quick release method to lower the pressure, and remove the lid.
8. Check the texture of the octopus with the tip of a sharp knife; it should be fork tender. If it's not cooked enough (highly unlikely) lock the lid back in place and cook it five minutes longer.
9. Using a slotted spoon, transfer the octopus to a bowl. Set 1 cup of the cooking liquid aside, reserving the rest for soup, stock, or sauce.
10. Return the pan with the onions to medium heat. Stir in the garlic and cook until it becomes aromatic, about a minute. Add the tomatoes, crushing them in your fingers before dropping them into the pan. Add half the tomato puree left in the can, half a cup of octopus cooking liquid, and the red pepper flakes. Allow the sauce to simmer for 15 minutes for the flavors to blend and the sauce to thicken. Add more octopus liquid if it seems too thick.
11. Add the octopus and simmer five more minutes. Taste and adjust the seasonings.
12. While the sauce is simmering, cook the penne in the pot of boiling water, using the manufacturer's suggested cooking time as a guide so it will finish at roughly the same time as the sauce.
13. Drain the cooked pasta, return it to the pot, and toss with the sauce.
14. Serve on warmed plates, garnished with the parsley.

🍸 KEN RIVARD
adapted from Lorna Sass's "Cooking Under Pressure" (HarperCollins)

ASK THE COOKS

Cold Pasta

Q Some people say to rinse pasta with cold water after cooking, so it doesn't stick together. Others say that rinsing doesn't do anything but make cold pasta. Who's right?

ANSWER Always boil pasta in plenty of salted water (6 quarts of water per pound of pasta). As the pasta cooks, some of its starch dissolves, causing the water to become cloudy. The more water, the less the concentration of starch, hence, nonstick pasta.

Rinsing may be helpful when making a pasta salad, because it will wash some starch from the surface and keep the pasta loose. Rinsing with cold water also will arrest the cooking process, or "shock" the pasta, so it does not become overdone.

When cooking pasta to be served hot, refrain from rinsing it. You might even add a little of the starchy cooking water to the finished sauce. Many cooks believe that the starch on the cooked pasta helps sauce adhere better. For that reason, I do not recommend adding oil to the cooking water. The oil will act like a nonstick coating, and all your sauce will end up in the bottom of the dish

☞ PETER J. KELLY

Scallop Ravioli with Pomegranates, Blood Oranges, and Brown Butter SERVES 4

8 tablespoons unsalted butter,
  at room temperature
1 teaspoon chopped fresh cilantro
1 teaspoon chopped fresh mint
1 teaspoon chopped fresh parsley
1/2 teaspoon ground coriander
1/8 teaspoon ground cumin
Kosher salt and freshly
  ground black pepper
4 large fresh dry (unbrined) sea scallops
1/4 cup semolina flour
  or fine cornmeal for dusting
24 2 1/2-inch pasta circles, or wonton
  wrappers cut into rounds
2 blood oranges
2 teaspoons minced shallots
1 teaspoon minced garlic
Freshly squeezed lemon juice, optional
2 tablespoons pomegranate seeds
4 teaspoons chopped, toasted pistachios
4 small bunches mache

1. In a bowl, combine 2 tablespoons butter with the cilantro, mint, parsley, coriander, and cumin. Beat until well combined, and season with salt and pepper. Form into a stubby log, wrap in plastic, and refrigerate the herb butter until solid.

2. Trim the tough muscle off the scallops. Cut each scallop into 3 slices and season with salt and pepper.

3. Lay out a sheet pan and cover with a tea towel. Sprinkle with semolina flour or cornmeal. This will hold the completed ravioli.

4. Lay half the pasta sheets out on a cutting board and brush the edges with water. Distribute the scallops between the rounds, arranging the shellfish in the centers. Cut the herb butter into 12 even pieces. Dot each scallop slice with a bit of herb butter. Top with the remaining pasta circles and seal well, pushing the air from the center out. Transfer to the tea towel.

5. Juice one of the blood oranges into a medium bowl. Working over the same bowl to catch any juice, cut the second orange into supremes — i.e. using a sharp knife, remove skin and pith, and remove the sections by cutting between the membranes. Put the supremes into a small bowl.

6. Melt the remaining butter in a medium sauté pan over medium heat. Cook for 5 minutes, or until the butter is nutty brown in color. Remove from the heat and reserve.

7. Bring a large pot of water to a boil, season with salt. Add the scallop ravioli and cook for 3-4 minutes, or until the ravioli float to the surface.

8. While the ravioli are cooking, put the pan with the butter back on a medium heat. Add the shallots and garlic and cook for 30 seconds, then add the blood orange juice and cook 30 seconds more and season with salt and pepper. Taste and adjust seasoning, adding a little lemon juice if the sauce seems too buttery or too rich.

9. Scoop the ravioli out of the water and into the brown butter sauce. Toss well and heat together for 30 seconds. Garnish with blood orange supremes, pomegranate seeds, pistachios, and mache.

▼ JODY ADAMS

JODY ADAMS
The award-winning chef of Rialto at the Charles Hotel in Cambridge, Massachusetts, describes her cuisine as "food I love to eat," so her menus incorporate French, Italian, Spanish, North African, and Middle Eastern cuisines. She has a 2002 cookbook, "In the Hands of a Chef" (Morrow Cookbooks), and is the culinary force behind The Sapphire Restaurant Group.

*"I love the dance of flavors and textures...
A simple New England scallop
s dressed to kill."*

lobster rolls

scallop burgers

shrimp BLTs with avocado

tuna on focaccia

lobster club

Sand

Some

Some people think of seafood as sophisticated fare. There's no better way to squelch that notion than to stuff it between two slices of bread — or into a hot dog roll, a particular favorite in these parts. Whether the seafood in question is mixed up with mayo, chopped or ground and shaped into a burger, or simply fried or grilled on its own, munching it in a sandwich takes it down a few notches on the formality scale. And somehow, it's more fun to eat when there are no knives or forks involved.

wiches

LOBSTER ROLLS

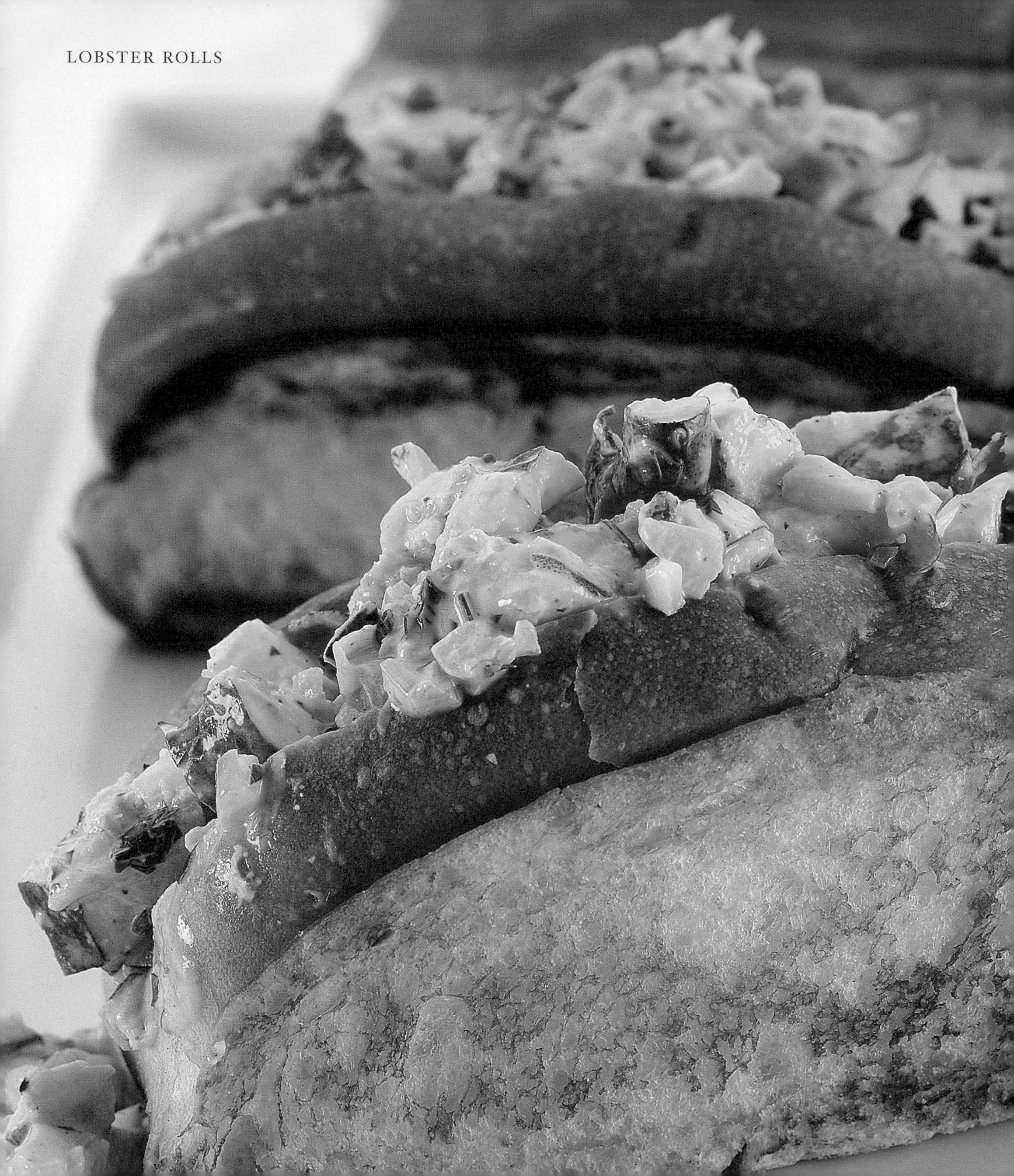

Starring Rolls

BY SHERYL JULIAN, Globe Staff,
and JULIE RIVEN, Globe Correspondent

New Englanders eat their lobster salad in hot dog rolls. We've been doing it for so long — and it's such prized eating in these parts — that we don't stop to realize how perfectly ridiculous this seems to outsiders. We actually take the luxurious meat of a freshly cooked lobster, mix it with commercial mayonnaise, and tuck it inside a golden brown, toasted ball-park bun. That formula flies out of beach-town clam shacks all summer.

Diehards know that the best roll for their seafood is an old-fashioned soft bread made from milk, egg, and a little butter, a roll that when fresh can be flattened to the thickness of a cookie with the heel of a hand. In July, they're in such demand that you can buy them in the drugstore.

Of course, they're incredibly good homemade. A homemade hot dog roll is a treasure. It's as good as the lobster filling tucked inside it. You can eat on the back porch and pretend you're dining at a clam-shack table. Imagine that the tide is going out and that the most important thing on your mind is making the lobster roll last as long as it can.

And when it's gone, get in the car and find some soft-serve ice cream. Some traditions should never change.

A homemade hot dog roll is a treasure. It's as good as the lobster filling tucked inside it. You can eat it on the back porch and pretend you're dining at a clam-shack table.

Lobster Rolls

SERVES 4

1 pound cooked lobster meat,
   cut into 1/2-inch pieces
2 stalks celery, finely chopped
4 scallions, finely chopped
1/4 cup chopped fresh parsley
1/2 cup mayonnaise
1/4 cup plain whole-milk yogurt
2 tablespoons lemon juice
1 teaspoon cayenne pepper
Salt and black pepper, to taste
4 hot dog rolls, pan-grilled in butter
   until golden

1. In a bowl, combine the lobster, celery, scallions, and parsley.
2. In a small bowl, mix together the mayonnaise, yogurt, lemon juice, cayenne pepper, salt, and black pepper. Stir well. Spoon the dressing over the lobster and mix thoroughly. Taste for seasoning and add more salt and pepper if you like.
3. Fill the rolls with lobster salad and serve at once.

❦ SHERYL JULIAN AND JULIE RIVEN

Hot Dog Rolls

MAKES 12

1 package active dry yeast
1/2 cup warm water
2 tablespoons sugar
3/4 cup warm whole milk
1 egg, lightly beaten
4 tablespoons (1/2 stick) melted butter
2 teaspoons salt
4 1/2 cups flour
Canola oil (for the bowl)
Extra flour (for sprinkling)
1 egg, lightly beaten (for the glaze)

1. In the bowl of an electric mixer fitted with the dough hook, or in a mixing bowl, sprinkle the yeast over the water. Add the sugar. Let the mixture stand for 10 minutes or until it begins to foam.
2. Stir in the milk, beaten egg, butter, and salt. Add 3 cups of the flour and mix thoroughly. Continue to add the remaining 1 1/2 cups of flour, a few large spoonfuls at a time, until the mixture comes together to form a dough. If using a mixer, continue kneading until the dough is smooth and elastic. If mixing by hand, turn the dough out onto a lightly floured counter and knead it until it is smooth and elastic.
3. Add a drop of oil to a clean bowl. Put the dough in it and turn it all around to cover it all over with oil. Cover the bowl with a damp towel and set the dough aside in a warm place for 1 1/2 hours or until it doubles in bulk.
4. Lightly grease a baking sheet or line it with parchment paper.
5. Turn the dough out onto a lightly floured counter. Punch it down and shape it into a log. Cut the dough into 12 pieces. Form each piece into a ball. One by one, roll a ball under your palms and shape it into a 6-inch-long oblong. Place it on the baking sheet. Set the next one 1/2 inch away, and so on, making 2 rows of 6 oblongs.
6. Cover the rolls with a cloth and set them aside for 1 hour or until they double in bulk. They will expand and touch.
7. Set the oven at 400 degrees. Brush the hot dog rolls with the beaten egg. Transfer the rolls to the hot

oven and bake them for 20 minutes or until the rolls are golden brown on top and hollow sounding when tapped at the bottom.
8. Remove the rolls from the oven and transfer them to a wire rack to cool. Use at once or store in plastic zipper bags until ready to use.
Note: For pan-grilled rolls, spread both sides with a faint coating of soft butter. Heat a cast-iron pan over medium heat for 1 minute and cook rolls on each side until golden brown.

❦ SHERYL JULIAN AND JULIE RIVEN

Cooke's Lobster Rolls

SERVES 4

It's hard not to smile when owner Spiro Mitrokostas greets you at the counter of Cooke's Seafood in Orleans, Massachusetts. An avid Red Sox fan with autographed player photos lining the walls of his roomy establishment, Mitrokostas makes conversation with everybody who passes by.

Cooke's menu includes lobster rolls (which some claim are the best on the Cape), fried shellfish and fish, grilled swordfish, hamburgers, and hot dogs. The fried clams here, which are frequently rated the best on the Cape by Cape Cod Life magazine, are addictively light and crunchy, with tender bellies.

Mitrokostas's generous lobster rolls are filled to bursting with chunks of fresh, sweet knuckle and claw meat, and a bit of mayonnaise, white vinegar, and white pepper, served on a bed of shredded lettuce in a buttered and toasted Pepperidge Farm hot dog bun.

1 to 1 1/2 pounds cooked lobster meat
(knuckles and claws),
cut into 1-inch pieces
4 tablespoons mayonnaise
1/2 teaspoon distilled white vinegar
White pepper, to taste
4 hot dog rolls (top-split)
1 tablespoon butter, melted
1/3 head iceberg lettuce, shredded

1. In a bowl, combine the lobster meat, mayonnaise, vinegar, and pepper.
2. Brush the sides of each hot dog roll with butter. Place the rolls, buttered side down, in a flat skillet over medium heat. Cook for 2 minutes or until golden brown. Turn the roll over and brown the other side.

3. Stand the rolls on 4 salad plates. Line the bottom of each roll with a bed of shredded lettuce. Divide the lobster evenly among the rolls.

Y ANDREA PYENSON
adapted from Cooke's Seafood

Grilled Tuna Salad Rolls
S E R V E S 4

Make this with leftover grilled or broiled fresh tuna, which you can turn into a salad with red onion, hard-cooked eggs, and a balsamic vinaigrette.

3 cups diced grilled or broiled tuna
1/2 red onion, finely chopped
2 hard-cooked eggs, coarsely chopped
2 ripe tomatoes, peeled, seeded,
and coarsely chopped

2 tablespoons capers, drained and chopped
1/4 cup torn basil leaves
Salt and pepper, to taste
2 tablespoons balsamic vinegar
1 tablespoon Dijon mustard
2 tablespoons olive oil
4 hot dog rolls, pan-grilled until golden

1. In a bowl, toss together the tuna, onion, eggs, tomatoes, capers, and basil.
2. In another bowl, whisk together the salt, pepper, and vinegar until the salt dissolves. Whisk in the mustard, followed by the oil, adding it 1 teaspoon at a time until the dressing emulsifies. Pour the dressing over the tuna mixture and toss thoroughly. Spoon the tuna into pan-grilled rolls and serve at once.
Note: The salad can be made several hours in advance and refrigerated until serving; the flavor will improve.

Y SHERYL JULIAN AND JULIE RIVEN

Snack Shacks

The outlet stores in Freeport, Maine, draw most folks off the Maine Turnpike like bees to honey. But for some of us, a visit to L.L. Bean or Abacus wouldn't be worth the drive if the itinerary didn't include a quick stop at a roadside stand for a boiled lobster or a lobster roll.

CINDY'S in Freeport has the perfect look of a Maine roadside stand. Improvised like the best jazz, it has lots of funny signs, picnic tables sheltered by umbrellas, and a Down East lobsterman atop the driveway sign. A vintage house trailer anchors the scene. A stand attached to the trailer is the place to order boiled lobsters and steamers. Another stand is cooking central for the rest of the

menu's chowder, fries, coleslaw, Indian pudding, and crab, clam, and lobster rolls. The lobster roll is tasty, a generous portion of small pieces and shredded meat. Cindy's is at 292 Route 1, Freeport, Maine. 207-865-1635. Open seasonally.
DAY'S CRABMEAT AND LOBSTER INC. in Yarmouth describes its creation as a whole lobster in a roll, and it certainly seems that way. The chunks and claws are

only lightly dressed with mayonnaise, so the meat's freshness stands out. Day's, housed in a white clapboard building, has a seafood market inside, while takeout orders are handled at outside windows. Picnic tables overlook the marsh, providing a place to sit and breathe in some salt air. Day's is at 1269 Route 1, Yarmouth, Maine. 207-846-5871. Open seasonally.
☛ JAN SHEPHERD

LOBSTER CLUB

Nice big chunks of lobster meat transform the traditional club sandwich into a New England classic.

Shrimp Salad Rolls
Ⓢ Ⓔ Ⓡ Ⓥ Ⓔ Ⓢ ④

Like the classic New England lobster roll, this salad of chopped shrimp, celery, and crumbled bacon, mixed with mayonnaise and sour cream, is heaped inside toasted hot dog rolls. Of course, you can also serve it on crusty bread.

1 1/2 pounds medium unshelled shrimp, thawed and soaked in cold salted water for 20 minutes
4 thick strips bacon
4 stalks celery, finely chopped
1/4 red onion, thinly sliced
1/4 cup chopped fresh parsley
1/2 cup mayonnaise, or to taste
2 tablespoons sour cream
2 teaspoons cider vinegar
Salt and pepper, to taste
4 hot dog rolls
2 tablespoons butter, softened at room temperature

1. Have on hand a large bowl of ice water. Bring a large pot of water to a brisk boil. Add the shrimp and, when the water returns to a boil, let the shrimp cook briskly for 1 minute or until they are cooked through. Drain the shrimp in a colander and plunge them into ice water.
2. When the shrimp are cold, drain and peel them. Chop them coarsely.
3. Transfer the shrimp to a bowl.
4. In a skillet, render the bacon in a dry pan over medium heat until the strips are golden. Transfer to a plate lined with paper towels. Blot the bacon to remove the excess fat. When the bacon is cool enough to handle, crumble it and add it to the shrimp. Add the celery, onion, and parsley.
5. In a small bowl, whisk together the mayonnaise and sour cream. Add the vinegar, 1/2 teaspoon at a time, until the mayonnaise mixture is smooth but still holds its shape. Spoon the mixture over the shrimp. Taste for seasoning and add salt and pepper if you like.
6. Spread the hot dog rolls with butter — you need just a small amount on each one. Heat a cast-iron skillet over medium heat and, when it is hot, add the rolls, buttered sides down, pressing them gently with a wide metal spatula until they are golden. Turn the rolls and brown the other sides.
7. Heap the shrimp salad inside the rolls and serve at once.
♈ SHERYL JULIAN AND JULIE RIVEN

Lobster Club Sandwich
Ⓢ Ⓔ Ⓡ Ⓥ Ⓔ Ⓢ ④

Besides donning a plastic bib and eating a boiled lobster until you and the table are a real mess, a true New England experience is lobster salad. This version is layered in a club sandwich with bacon, lettuce, and tomato.

4 thick strips bacon
1 1/4 pounds fresh lobster meat (from 2 1 1/2-pound lobsters), coarsely cut into small pieces
1/4 sweet onion, finely chopped
1 stalk celery, finely chopped
4 tablespoons mayonnaise
1 tablespoon sour cream
1 teaspoon lemon juice, or to taste
Salt and pepper, to taste
12 slices sandwich bread, lightly toasted
Extra mayonnaise (for spreading)
2 large ripe tomatoes, cored and thinly sliced
4 leaves Boston lettuce, cored and halved

1. Set a small skillet over medium-high heat and render the bacon until it is crisp and brown. Transfer the bacon to a plate lined with paper towels. Blot the bacon on both sides to absorb excess fat. Set the bacon aside.
2. In a small bowl, combine the lobster meat, onion, and celery.
3. In another bowl, combine the mayonnaise, sour cream, lemon juice, salt, and pepper. Stir well until the mixture is smooth. Add the lobster mixture to the mayonnaise mixture and stir gently but thoroughly. Taste for seasoning and add more lemon juice or salt if you like.
4. Set the toasted bread on the counter. Spread a light layer of mayonnaise on the 12 slices of toast. Top 4 of the slices with tomatoes, bacon, and lettuce. Cover each with another slice of toast, mayonnaise side up. Spoon some of the lobster salad on each of the sandwiches and close them with the remaining slices of toast, mayonnaise side down. Serve at once.
♈ SHERYL JULIAN AND JULIE RIVEN

Sandwich Loaf with Cream Cheese Frosting

SERVES 8

Moms in the 1950s did a lot of cooking off the packages in their pantry. It was a good system, actually. Food corporations spent money developing recipes using their products, and housewives depended upon them. Anyone who made a recipe from the back of a box knew that it would be a success.

This is where a host of cream cheese recipes originated. Cocktail parties invariably included a cheese ball or a hot crab dip. Sandwich loaf is a fantastic creation that begins with lengthwise slices of white bread spread with various sandwich fillings, reshaped to form a rectangular cake, then covered all over with cream cheese "frosting." No 1950s party was complete without one.

TUNA SALAD LAYER

1 can (6 ounces) light tuna in oil, drained
1 tablespoon drained sweet pickle relish
3 tablespoons mayonnaise
1 small stalk celery, finely chopped

1. In the bowl of a food processor, work the tuna in on-off motions until it is coarsely chopped. Add the relish and mayonnaise and pulse a few times until smooth.

Remove the processor cover and scrape down the bowl as necessary. Add the celery and pulse again until it is blended.
2. Transfer the mixture to a bowl. Wipe out the food processor.

SALMON LAYER

1/4 medium red onion
2 tablespoons fresh dill leaves
1 can (7 1/2 ounces) red salmon, drained (skin and bones removed)
2 tablespoons mayonnaise

1. In the bowl of the food processor, work the onion and dill until coarsely chopped.
2. Add the salmon and pulse to chop it coarsely. Add the mayonnaise and continue to pulse the mixture until it is smooth. Remove the processor cover and scrape down the bowl as necessary.
3. Transfer the mixture to a bowl. Wipe out the food processor.

OLIVE LAYER

1/2 jar (4 ounces) pimento-stuffed olives, drained
4 ounces (1/2 of an 8-ounce package) cream cheese, at room temperature

1. In the bowl of the food processor, coarsely chop the olives.
2. Cut up the cream cheese and add it to the processor. Pulse the mixture just until smooth. Transfer the olive filling to a bowl.

FOR THE LOAF

1 loaf unsliced sandwich bread or square challah, cut lengthwise into 8 slices
2 packages (8 ounces each) cream cheese, at room temperature

2 to 4 tablespoons whole milk, or enough to soften the frosting
Pimento-stuffed olives (for garnish)
Italian parsley (for garnish)

1. Remove 6 of the middle slices of the loaf. Reserve the outside slices for another use.
2. Place 1 slice lengthwise on the counter. Spread half the tuna salad on it and cover with another slice.
3. Spread half of the salmon salad on the second slice. Add a third slice of bread and cover it with all of the olive spread.
4. Add a fourth slice of bread and cover it with the remaining salmon. Add a fifth slice of bread, and then the remaining tuna. Cover with the sixth slice of bread. Carefully transfer the layered loaf to a platter.
5. Cover with plastic wrap and refrigerate while you prepare the frosting.
6. In an electric mixer, beat the cream cheese, scraping down the sides of the bowl and adding the milk, 1 teaspoon at a time, until it is fluffy. With a flexible metal palette knife, frost the layers all over with the cream cheese mixture. Refrigerate for about 2 hours or until cold.
7. To serve, use a sharp serrated knife to cut the loaf into thick slices. Garnish with olives and parsley. Use a wide metal spatula to transfer the slices to small plates. Serve with forks.

To make a day in advance: Place a toothpick in each of the corners of the sandwich loaf. Wrap the loaf in plastic wrap — the toothpicks prevent sticking — and refrigerate.
▼ SHERYL JULIAN AND JULIE RIVEN

Coolers

Coolers now come in a range of shapes, sizes, and materials. Some are built like golf bags, others like soft-sided square duffels. They all do a decent job at their most basic function. So if you're in the market, imagine what you'll use the cooler for and let the occasion dictate.

Igloo MaxCold 40 (www. igloo-store.com): Sturdy large wheels make it as easy to roll as a kid's wagon. Good for camping. A bit large for true portability.

Coleman Ultimate Extreme 70 (www.coleman.com): Huge capacity makes it perfect for parties; easy-drain system is a nice touch. Too bulky for smaller tasks, since it requires about 50 pounds of ice for proper cooling.

Brookstone Portable Auto Fridge (www.brookstone.com): Fits between bucket seats of car, and uses cigarette lighter socket instead of ice. Limited to car use; awkward to carry.

Igloo Collapsible 54 (www. igloo-store.com): With telescoping handle and wheels, plus collapsibility, it's suited for air travel. Small capacity makes it useful for errands, but not events.

Kelsyus Backpack Cooler (www.swimways.com/kelsyus): The ultimate in portability; separate sections make it great for beachgoing and hiking. Cooler section holds 8 cans: enough space for a meal for two, but not much more. ✒ JOE YONAN

Caramelized Onion, Tuna, and Black Olive on Focaccia

SERVES 6

Many pizza parlors sell their spongy uncooked dough by the pound, a fine substitute for these recipes. When time is short, you can buy it ready-made, pat it out, and make something that will become your standby summer meal.

2 tablespoons olive oil
2 large Spanish onions,
    halved and thinly sliced
Salt and black pepper, to taste
Pinch of sugar
1 store-bought or homemade focaccia,
    cut into 6 pieces
1 can or jar (6 to 8 ounces) tuna
    in olive oil, drained and flaked
2 tablespoons capers, drained
1/4 cup cured black olives,
    pitted and coarsely chopped
Pinch of crushed red pepper (optional)

1. In a large skillet, heat the oil. Add the onions, salt, and black pepper and cook over medium heat, stirring often, for 15 minutes. Add a pinch of sugar and continue to cook for 15 minutes, stirring often, or until the onions are almost jam-like.

2. Slice focaccia pieces in half. Layer one side of the pieces with onions. Add tuna, capers, olives, and red pepper, if using. Close the sandwiches and serve at once.
✒ SHERYL JULIAN AND JULIE RIVEN

Focaccia

MAKES 6 PIECES

If you like, you can mix the dough and refrigerate it in a covered container overnight. Cold dough is easier to roll, but you will need to add 10 to 15 minutes to the second rising time.

2 teaspoons dried yeast
1 teaspoon sugar
3/4 cup lukewarm water
3 1/2 cups flour
2 teaspoons salt
2 tablespoons olive oil
1/4 cup milk
Olive oil (for sprinkling)

1. In a small bowl, stir together the yeast, sugar, and warm water. Set the mixture aside for 10 minutes or until it is frothy.

2. In the bowl of a food processor, pulse the flour and salt just to sift them. Add the yeast mixture, oil, and milk. Work the processor in on-off motions just until the mixture forms a smooth ball.

3. Oil a large bowl. Place the dough in the bowl and turn it in the oil to coat it all over. Cover the bowl with plastic wrap and set it aside in a warm place for 2 hours or until the dough has doubled in bulk.

4. Punch the dough down. Set it on a work surface and knead gently for 2 minutes. Roll the dough out to a 10-inch round. If it is difficult to roll, cover it with a cloth and let it sit for a few minutes. Then continue rolling.

5. Cut the dough into 6 triangular wedges.

6. Lightly oil a rimmed baking sheet or line it with parchment paper. Set the round or wedges on the sheet. Cover with a cloth and set aside in a warm place for 30 minutes to rise.

7. Set the oven at 400 degrees. Sprinkle the focaccia lightly with oil. Bake for 15 to 20 minutes or until lightly brown and firm to the touch. Remove from the oven and set on a wire rack to cool.

❦ SHERYL JULIAN AND JULIE RIVEN

Shrimp BLTs with Smashed Avocados

Ⓢ Ⓔ Ⓡ Ⓥ Ⓔ Ⓢ ④

There's a season for everything. Even in New England in mid-winter, there's a brief opportunity to taste one of the true local seafood delicacies of the region: tiny, bright pink, deliciously juicy Maine shrimp.

These shrimp are sweet and crisp and only hours out of the sea. Grilling experts Chris Schlesinger and John Willoughby like to grill their shrimp and toss them with smashed avocados in a BLT. With tiny Maine shrimp, use a broiler instead, and add the same smoky and crisp garnishes.

1 pound Maine shrimp, peeled
Salt and pepper, to taste
Olive oil (for sprinkling)
2 ripe avocados, peeled, pitted, and cut into dice
2 tablespoons chopped red onion
Juice of 1 1/2 limes, or to taste
Dash of liquid hot sauce

8 slices sandwich bread, lightly toasted
12 slices bacon, cooked crisp
4 leaves romaine lettuce
2 tomatoes, sliced 1/2-inch thick

1. Turn on the broiler. Sprinkle the shrimp with salt and pepper and toss with enough oil to coat them.

2. Broil the shrimp for 2 minutes, turning once, or until they are cooked through. Cool to lukewarm.

3. In a bowl, toss the avocados, shrimp, onion, lime juice, hot sauce, salt, and pepper. The mixture should form a thick and chunky kind of paste.

4. Put a generous mound of shrimp mixture on each of 4 pieces of bread. Add bacon, lettuce, and tomato. Sandwich with the top slices.

❦ ALISON ARNETT
adapted from Chris Schlesinger and John Willoughby's "Big Flavors of the Hot Sun" (Morrow)

Marinated Squid Sandwich with Slaw

Ⓢ Ⓔ Ⓡ Ⓥ Ⓔ Ⓢ ④

1 pound squid
Olive oil (for sprinkling)
Salt and pepper, to taste
Juice of 1 lemon
1 tablespoon Dijon mustard
1 tablespoon chopped fresh thyme
1/4 cup olive oil

1. Turn on the broiler. Slice the squid thinly into 1/4-inch-thick rings. Leave the tentacles whole if they are small, or halve them. Place the squid on a rack in a broiling pan.

2. Sprinkle the squid with olive oil, salt, and pepper. Broil the squid as close to the element as possible, cooking it for 2 minutes or until it is just cooked through. Remove the squid from the oven and transfer it to a bowl.

3. In another bowl, combine the lemon juice with salt and pepper. Stir in the mustard and thyme. Slowly pour in the olive oil, whisking constantly, until the dressing emulsifies. Pour the dressing over the squid and toss it thoroughly.

SLAW
1/2 cup mayonnaise
2 tablespoons cider vinegar
Pinch of sugar
Salt and pepper, to taste
1 small red cabbage, cored and thinly sliced
1 English cucumber, peeled, seeded, and thinly sliced
1/2 red onion, very thinly sliced
4 large radishes, very thinly sliced
8 slices whole-wheat bread
4 large leaves of leaf lettuce

1. In a small bowl, whisk together the mayonnaise, vinegar, sugar, salt, and pepper.

2. In a large bowl, toss together the cabbage, cucumber, onion, and radishes. Pour the dressing over the vegetables and toss thoroughly. Cover tightly and refrigerate for up to 1 hour.

3. Set a slice of bread on each of 4 dinner plates. Add cabbage and squid. Cover with lettuce and the remaining slices of bread. Transfer the remaining slaw to a serving dish.

❦ SHERYL JULIAN AND JULIE RIVEN

SALMON BURGER

Salmon Burgers with Sour Cream Dill Sauce

SERVES 4

Americans like their patties made with any ground meat — even fish — that will hold together with a few breadcrumbs. The patties need to be firm enough to sear in a skillet (these are fragile, so handle them carefully). Then tuck them inside a bun or between slices of toast or into a pita pocket.

1 1/4-pound piece boneless salmon
Canola oil (for sprinkling and frying)
Salt and pepper, to taste
1 clove garlic, quartered
1/4 cup fresh parsley leaves
2 slices white sandwich bread, torn up
1 egg, lightly beaten
1/4 cup mayonnaise
Flour (for sprinkling)
1/2 red onion, thinly sliced (for garnish)

1. Turn on the broiler. Set the salmon, skin side down, in a baking dish. Sprinkle it lightly with oil, salt, and pepper. Broil the fish for 10 minutes, without turning, or until it is cooked through. Set it aside to cool.
2. Remove and discard the fish skin and any fatty pieces from the salmon. In a shallow bowl with a fork, flake the fish.
3. In a food processor, work the garlic, parsley, and bread until they are fine. Transfer the mixture to the salmon. Add the egg and mayonnaise and with the fork, blend the mixture until it is smooth.
4. Divide the mixture into 4 patties, shaping them gently with flour.
5. In a large nonstick skillet, heat enough oil to make a very thin layer. When it is hot, add the burgers and cook over medium-high heat, turning once, for 6 to 8 minutes or until they are golden brown and hot.
6. Arrange the burgers on each of 4 plates, garnish with onion slices, and add dill sauce.

SAUCE

1/2 cup sour cream
3 tablespoons chopped fresh dill
1 tablespoon lemon juice
Salt and pepper

In a bowl, mix together the sour cream, dill, lemon juice, salt, and pepper. Cover with plastic wrap and refrigerate.

🍸 SHERYL JULIAN AND JULIE RIVEN

Scallop Burgers

SERVES 4

Because fish cakes were traditionally made with leftover fish, the fish was always cooked. However, that's no longer the case, and it may be why some people refer to fish cakes as fish burgers. "A fish cake is a fish burger and vice versa," says Jane Murphy, coauthor of "The Great Big Burger Book." The book's so-called "burgers from the sea" contain chopped or ground fish, with about half of the recipes calling for uncooked fish.

Serve the burgers on toasted buns with tartar sauce or a spicy mayonnaise.

2 tablespoons olive oil
1/2 cup peeled celeriac cut into 1/4-inch dice, or chopped celery
2 tablespoons mayonnaise
1 teaspoon Dijon mustard
1/2 teaspoon Worcestershire sauce
1 pound sea scallops, finely chopped
1 tablespoon finely chopped chives
1 large egg, lightly beaten
1 cup panko or plain dry bread crumbs
1/2 teaspoon kosher salt

1. In a large skillet, heat 1/2 tablespoon of olive oil over moderate heat. Cook the celeriac, stirring for 5 minutes or until softened. Transfer the celeriac into a large bowl.
2. In a small bowl, mix together the mayonnaise, mustard, and Worcestershire sauce.
3. To the bowl with the celeriac, add the scallops, mayonnaise mixture, chives, egg, panko, and salt. Mix thoroughly. Form into 4 patties, each about 3/4-inch thick. Refrigerate on a plate, covered with plastic wrap, for 30 minutes.
4. In the same skillet, heat the remaining 1 1/2 tablespoons of oil over medium-high heat. Add the patties and cook until brown on the bottom, about 3-4 minutes. Turn and cook the other side 2-4 minutes.

🍸 LISA ZWIRN
adapted from Jane Murphy and Liz Yeh Singh's "The Great Big Burger Book" (Harvard Common Press)

Open-Faced Crab and Asparagus Sandwich

SERVES 2

4 bacon strips
Vegetable oil
2 large, fresh, spring-dug parsnips
Flour, for dusting parsnips
2 thick slices of brioche, challah,
  or Portuguese bread
4 jumbo spears asparagus
3 tablespoons butter
1/2 cup fresh Maine crabmeat
1 teaspoon parsley or chives,
  chopped
2 egg yolks
1/2 teaspoon grated blood orange rind
2 tablespoons strained blood orange juice
1 teaspoon lemon juice
1/2 teaspoon salt
Pinch of cayenne pepper
10 tablespoons butter, melted and still hot
2 eggs
Kosher salt and freshly
  ground black pepper to taste

1. Set the oven at 350 degrees.
2. On a cookie sheet, lay bacon on top of parchment paper. Cover the bacon with a second sheet of parchment paper and weigh it down with a heavy flat-bottomed pan so the bacon won't buckle. Roast in the oven until crisp, approximately 15 minutes. Set aside to cool on a wire rack.
3. Fill a Dutch oven or deep pot half way with vegetable oil and heat to 325 degrees.
4. Peel spring-dug parsnips in long strips. Dust strips lightly with flour and fry until crisp and a touch golden. Remove from oil with slotted spoon and place on paper towels to drain. Sprinkle with a touch of salt. Set aside.
5. Toast bread in the oven for about 4 minutes, until light golden.
6. Starting three inches from the top of each asparagus spear, lightly peel to the base of the stalk (leaving the top unpeeled). Place the asparagus in a small sauté pan with salted water just barely covering the vegetable. Boil rapidly over high heat until water is gone and asparagus is tender. Add 1 tablespoon of butter to "glisten" the asparagus. Set aside.
7. In a small sauté pan, melt 2 tablespoons butter over medium heat. When the butter is sizzling, add crabmeat. When the crabmeat is warmed, sprinkle with parsley or chives.
8. Make a blood orange hollandaise: In an electric blender, place 2 egg yolks, blood orange rind, blood orange juice, lemon juice, 1/2 teaspoon salt, and cayenne pepper, and blend at slow speed for two minutes. Then slowly pour in 10 tablespoons of hot melted butter. Taste for seasoning and set aside in a warm space.
9. Assemble the sandwiches: Turn the oven down to 300 degrees. Place toasted bread on heated plates. Crisscross two asparagus spears on each piece of toast. Spoon crabmeat on top of the asparagus. Place in the oven for two minutes to warm through. Meanwhile, cook two eggs sunnyside up in a tiny square skillet, making sure that the yolk is not cooked through. If you can't get your hands on a square skillet, fry the egg as you normally would and trim to square off the rounded edges of the cooked egg-white. Remove plates from the oven, slide egg on top, sprinkle with salt and pepper. Spoon a heaping tablespoon of hollandaise on top and serve immediately with bacon and parsnip chips.

 LYDIA SHIRE

LYDIA SHIRE
With her award-winning cuisine at Seasons, Biba, Pignoli, and Locke Ober, Shire has been instrumental in putting Boston on the gastronomic map. Her limitless creativity and commitment to hard work have earned her high praise, including Best Chef/Northeast honors from the James Beard Foundation, and the prestigious Ivy Award for up-and-coming trendsetters. She's a true New England original.

"I found a 4-inch-square Griswold egg skillet at a flea market and couldn't wait to cook a square egg in it."

Recipe Index

PHOTO, PREVIOUS PAGE: At daybreak, there's already a line for fishing striped bass along Parsons Beach in Kennebunk, Maine.